THE WINEMAKER'S YEAR

·············· FOUR SEASONS IN ··············

Bordeaux

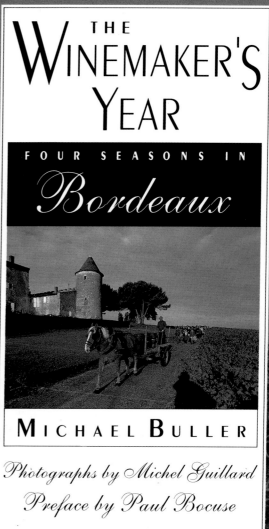

THE
WINEMAKER'S
YEAR

FOUR SEASONS IN
Bordeaux

MICHAEL BULLER

Photographs by Michel Guillard
Preface by Paul Bocuse

THAMES AND HUDSON

First published in the United States in 1991 by

Thames and Hudson Inc., 500 Fifth Avenue, New York, New York 10110

First published in Great Britain in 1991 by

Thames and Hudson Ltd, London

Produced by Laura Cerwinske Editorial Production

New York, New York

Library of Congress Catalogue Card Number 91-65286

Art directed and designed by Beth Tondreau Design

Printed in Singapore

Emile Peynaud • *Henri Martin* • *to Daniel Querre* • *and to their children*
....

This book was made possible thanks to many along the road who have given me so much of themselves. In particular, the winemakers of Bordeaux and Saint Emilion whose words are the book; and who, with their families, have been my family all these years.

Professeur Emile Peynaud

Henri Martin, Château Gloria and Château Saint-Pierre

Alexis Lichine, Château Prieuré-Lichine

Jean-Paul Gardère, Château Latour

Jean-Eugène Borie, Château Ducru-Beaucaillou

Laura and Corinne Mentzelopoulos, Château Margaux

Comte Alexandre and Comtesse Berangère de Lur-Saluces, Château Yquem

Baron Eric de Rothschild, Château Lafite-Rothschild

Baron Philippe de Rothschild, Château Mouton-Rothschild

Peter Alan Sichel, Château Angludet and Château Palmer

Jean-Bernard Delmas, Château Haut-Brion

Michel Delon, Château Léoville-Las-Cases

Jean-Michel Cazes, Château Lynch-Bages

Peter M.F. Sichel, Château Fourcas-Hostens

Bruno Prats, Château Cos d'Estournel

André Lurton, Château Bonnet

Sophie Schyler, Château Kirwan

Jean Cruse, Château La Dame Blanche

Martin Bamford, Château Loudenne

Ronald and Anthony Barton, Château Langoa-Barton

Pierre Tari, Château Giscours

Claude Ricard, Domaine de Chevalier

Alfred Tesseron, Château Pontet Canet

Edouard Kressman, Château La Tour Martillac

Pierre Perromat, President, I.N.A.O.

Jean-Michel Courteau, CIVB

Jacques Boissoneau

Jacques Hébrard, Château Cheval Blanc

Mme Jean Dubois-Challon, Château Ausone

Daniel and Alain Querre, Château Monbousquet

Jean-Pierre and Christian Moueix, Château Magdelaine and Château Pétrus, Pomerol

Eric Fournier, Château Canon

Jean-Paul Valette, Château Pavie

Pascal Delbeck, Château Belair

Thierry Manoncourt, Château Figeac

Dominique Lurton, Clos Fourtet

Comte Leo Malet de Roquefort, Château La Gaffelière

Emile and Philippe Casteja, Château Trottevieille

Dr. Pierre Duffau-Lagarrosse, Château Beausejour (Duffau-Lagarrosse)

Jean Meneret, Château Larmande

Guy and Simone Thoilliez, Château Puyrazac

Jacques-Antoine Baugier, Union des Producteurs de St. Emilion

Syndicat Vinicole de Saint Emilion; Jurade of Saint Emilion

For beautifully capturing the setting for this book, I must thank a dear friend, *the* photographer of Bordeaux, Michel Guillard. And for kindly watching, correcting, encouraging, I thank Peter M.F. Sichel.

Finally, special thanks to my publisher, Peter Warner, who had a vision of the book. I thank him for his understanding, clear eye and encouragement. And with him, the editor, Laura Cerwinske, and the designer, Beth Tondreau.

Spring · 18

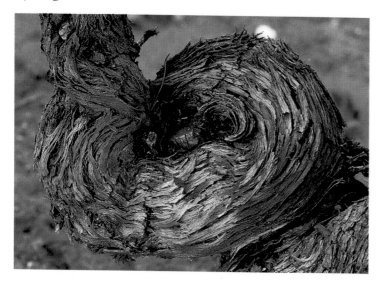

Summer · 46

 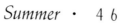

Contents

7

Preface

BY

Paul Bocuse

Lyon and Bordeaux are the centers of greatly privileged regions of France. Just as my own region around Lyon is considered the nation's larder, so the Bordeaux country is the home of great wine cellars and vineyards respected the world over. As well as wines, Bordeaux also offers some fine regional cuisine and local produce—*foie gras* from the Périgord and the Landes. The three rivers of Bordeaux are renowned for fish such as lamprey and shad; the Médoc peninsula for its lamb, which traditionally graze on the low-lying countryside; and the port of Arcachon on the Atlantic for its oysters.

As a young chef, I was an apprentice in the kitchen of Fernand Point's restaurant near Lyon. A big man, he was proud of his cellar, and his list of Bordeaux wines was one of the finest in the region. My colleague Jean Troisgros and I learned from Point the importance of visiting the market every day to select the produce and stay in contact with the producers. We also learned that it is equally important for the chef and restaurateur to make frequent visits to the vineyard. Bordeaux was one of our favorite pilgrimages.

Our friends the winemakers came to dine in our restaurants, or we met them on overseas journeys—often at tastings and wine "summits" assembled by Michael Buller. He has been our ambassador and one of the first to understand the relationship and alliance of the winemaker and the chef at these occasions. We found ourselves more frequently meeting in Texas, New York, or London than in Lyon and Bordeaux.

Just as he became one of the family of winemakers, Michael became one of our family of chefs too. He ate at the table in our kitchen, accompanied us to the market, traveled with us, listened, and recorded our stories.

Just as my father, just as Fernand Point, Henri Martin, Emile Peynaud, Daniel Querre, and others passed on the message to us, it is important that the message is passed on today to future generations.

Introduction

THE ROAD TO
BORDEAUX
BY
Michael Buller

I went to France in 1955 for three weeks and stayed for fifteen years. At the invitation of friends, I left London for Paris where I became a reporter for the French state radio. At the same time I joined the administration of Jean Vilar and Gerard Philipe's French National Theatre—Gerard Philipe and Maria Casares were the stars, Maurice Jarre was composer and conductor, and our summer home was the Palace of the Popes at Avignon. Paris was the world's marketplace for art, fashion, film, theatre, and music hall—the world of Edith Piaf, Yves Montand, Jacques Brel, and Georges Brassens.

My personal Paris was the weekly visits to the street markets for fresh vegetables and fruit; the store filled with cheeses and butter where I went for my daily can of fresh milk; the smell of baking bread rising from the bakery on the walk home after the theatre, the same bakery that cooked my Christmas turkey. With the food, came the wine: the bottle of *vin ordinaire* refilled at the local grocer's; the glass on the counter in the bar; the carafe of the *patron's* house wine with the midnight bowl of onion soup after the broadcast; and the château bottle with the beautiful label bought at Christmastime.

In 1964 I moved to Bordeaux to work for one of its oldest houses of wine merchants and shippers, with offices and cellars on the Chartrons quayside. The firm was governed by a board of twelve, three generations of the Cruse family. Their leader, Jean Cruse—a kind, elegant man with white side-whiskers, the stature of a general, and a château, La Dame Blanche, straight out of *Gone With the Wind*—headed a group of château owners and shippers who determined the prices and world allocation of five of the First Growths, the top châteaux of Bordeaux. My first steps on the wine road were spent accompanying him when he showed visitors the family châteaux in the Médoc.

I lived in a world of wine merchants—shippers, wine brokers, château

*Ships on the Gironde estuary,
above and opposite.*

owners, cellar masters, and winegrowers. The wine at the châteaux and shippers' cellars was made by the cellar master under the supervision of the owners. In Bordeaux the tradition of winemaking passed from father to son. In those days, I saw no sign of the man we call today the winemaker. He was not in the cellars or dark, oak-lined corridors of the châteaux, not at table in the dining rooms overlooking the vineyards, never mentioned in the books on wine in the châteaux' libraries.

One day I asked my employers if I might attend the Monday morning oenology classes of Professor Emile Peynaud at the University of Bordeaux. Oenology, the science of winemaking, had been largely created by Louis Pasteur in the nineteenth century, and by Jean Ribereau-Gayon and Emile Peynaud over the last fifty years. Coming out of Peynaud's class, I would pass the winegrowers, with their ruddy, weather-bitten complexions, sitting outside his office, clasping their sample bottles in their hands, like owners of pets outside the veterinarian's door. They had found the winemaker. And so had I.

Emile Peynaud, the winemaker's winemaker, was born in Bordeaux in 1912. At the age of sixteen, on his father's death, he began to earn a living rolling barrels in the cellars of one of the wine houses and working at the university under Professor Ribereau-Gayon (whose grandfather had collaborated with Pasteur). He became the director of research at the Center of Oenology at the university—retiring in 1977 after a twenty-five-year collaboration with Ribereau-Gayon. By the 1970s he was consultant to a hundred châteaux, shippers, and cooperatives of Bordeaux—which at one time represented a fifth of the region's annual production. His influence on the winemaker is to be found throughout this book.

I remember his words: "The wine of Bordeaux is a wine of rivers." Two rivers—the Dordogne, which flows down from the Massif Central of France, and the Garonne, which originates in the Pyrenees along the Franco-Spanish border—meet just below the port of Bordeaux where they become the Gironde estuary. At Pauillac—opposite Château Latour—the estuary is ten miles wide. These rivers provide the temperate climate and mass of humid air that protect the soils. The vineyards, planted on hillsides that run along the rivers, are healthy from natural drainage. "Every important wine region in Europe is situated near a river," says Peynaud. "You need a lot of water to make a good wine."

Bordeaux, in southwestern France, is only fifty miles from the Atlantic Ocean and the sailing port of Arcachon, site of some of France's finest oyster beds. It is one of the rare red wine regions to be directly influenced by the Atlantic climate; to the north there are no red wines, and to the south, along the northern Spanish coastline, there are no wines. Further south, Portugal, with its port wines, is not influenced by the Atlantic. One has to go as far south as South Africa to find another wine region touched by the Atlantic.

With some thirty-five or forty wine districts or place names, *appellations,* not to mention the thousands of château names, even the people of Bordeaux are often confused by so many names. Peynaud has devised his own simple map of Bordeaux. "I describe the districts by the rivers: the wines of the River Garonne, the wines of the River Dordogne, and the wines of the Gironde estuary. Each are of a different character due to the different nature of the soil. On the left bank of the Garonne and the Gironde are gravelly soils we call *graves* (hence the name of the region). Their sand and stone came down from the Massif Central in huge rivers at the end of the Ice Age, leaving a layer of soil that is often several meters deep, which forces the roots to dig far down to find water and food for the vine. The roots thrive on this fight for existence. So poor and meager are these soils that a famous nineteenth-century chemist, unfamiliar with the region, once concluded that the soil at Château Lafite-Rothschild was 'unfit for cultivating the vine.'"

Archaeological excavations have revealed that small vineyards in Bordeaux existed since the time of the Roman Occupation, around A.D. 43, when the vines were probably transported from Italy and brought up the river valleys. The early vineyards around the city of Bordeaux produced wines for the

The highly porous, gravelly soils of the region, above and right.

citizens. As the vineyards developed, the wine had to be marketed. "A region with a large production of wine can only exist if there is a well organized wine trade," explains Peynaud, "and a region's development is possible when the trade becomes powerful and strong. One does not first plant the vines and then look for where to sell the wine. Trade exists because of demand. *Le négoce,* the wine trade of Bordeaux, created the region of Bordeaux, not the winegrowers."

The early Bordeaux wine merchants quickly realized the importance of the rivers. By the Middle Ages, the Bordeaux wine trade had so developed that they were shipping wines to the countries of Northern Europe and to the British Isles. During the three hundred years of the English occupation of Aquitaine, from 1154 to 1453, the English wine fleet would sail down to Bordeaux. Each October and February two hundred ships anchored in the port. Once loaded with barrels of wine, they took from a week to two months to sail back to London, depending on the weather. Along the way they stopped to pick up barrels of cognac at the mouth of the Gironde. "Cognac, port, and sherry were created *by* the English, *for* the English," says Peynaud.

The wines from the region of the Dordogne river were also exported—but by the wine trade at the port of Libourne. Until the nineteenth century, the wines on the other side of the river—from Bourg and Blaye to Saint Emilion, Pomerol, and Fronsac—were not familiar in Bordeaux. After Napoleon built the first bridges across the Dordogne and the Garonne in 1809 to enable his troops to cross down into Spain to fight against the Duke of Wellington and the English army in the Peninsular War, Bordeaux started to trade the wines of Saint Emilion.

The great period of the creation of the Bordeaux châteaux and vineyards we know today dates from the eighteenth century. "This is when we began to know techniques better, transport became easier, the glass industry developed bottles, and the manufacture of corks improved in quality," Peynaud explains. "Corks had been used since Roman times, but their use in preserving wine in a bottle for a long time was a technique that only saw the light of day in the eighteenth century."

This was also an age of refinement of taste. "A *grand vin* can only exist if there are wine lovers who are aware, enlightened, and able to spend more money to have something a little better," says Peynaud.

An illustration from a medieval book of hours showing workers in the vineyards, top. An eighteenth-century engraving of le négoce, *above.*

....

Grape-picking baskets lined up and awaiting use, right. Opposite, the bell tower of Saint Emilion rising above the town.

This book is drawn from twenty-five years with the winemakers of Bordeaux. Walking with them through their vineyards and cellars, sitting at their tables and listening, I recorded this oral history of a countryside and a way of life. The voice of the winemaker in the book is made up of many winemakers, a story told here *in their words* for the first time.

I have had a lasting love affair with Bordeaux. To this day I still return regularly to walk along the deserted quaysides in the early morning mists. I pass the cellars stretching back, street after street, behind the façades of the wine houses. I drive out into the vineyards in winter with the winds beating down on the bare vines. On warmer days, I seek out a vineyard along the banks of the Gironde and watch the ships sailing down to the ocean. Henri Martin of Château Gloria once told me, "You have been marked for life by Bordeaux."

Spring

"As a matter of habit, I am always up by six-thirty," says Alain Querre, winemaker and proprietor of Château Monbousquet on a spring morning. "The bedroom windows are open, so the light of day enters. Even in winter, when the mornings are dark, I am up at the same time. Going downstairs to let out my dogs, I hear the birds having a concert. They are more awake than I am. By evening I am more awake than they are as they have gone to bed; they are quiet and I can hear everything— even the insects in the air. But at six-thirty in the morning, the birds outside are making great music. It is the New Orleans jazz band!"

Querre, like most of the winemakers we will meet, inherited the art of winemaking from his father, Daniel, a solid, full-bodied man still remembered fondly in Saint Emilion. With some sixty-nine acres of vineyards, Monbousquet produces about 175,000 bottles of red wine each year.

Spring is a time of reawakening and rebirth, and a good time for Querre to introduce us to the world of Bordeaux's winemakers. This world is not simply a region, nor a sophisticated agricultural enterprise, but a way of life, a tradition that is still pursued with passion and conviction.

"My manager, Thoilliez, sees to everything," says Querre as we drive to his vineyard manager's office at the château, a sparse room with a table, chair, and a large plan of the château and its vineyards stretched across one wall. The two men run through the day's work.

"Although he is in command, he likes to have my approval, my support," continues Querre as we walk across to the pressing house. "If there is a little time, I may go on a tour with him around the property, practically the same round as I did with my father for twenty-five years. Times haven't changed so much around here."

The first buds, above, and a winegrower's wife hanging her laundry, opposite.

Dawn in the vineyards.

The workers are on their way out to the vineyards. This is time for the second plowing, for uncovering the bases of the vines that have been protected through winter, and for replanting parts of the vineyard.

"At this hour of the day," says Querre, "I am usually too busy to stop and appreciate nature, although I'm aware of the mists mounting over the vines and the sun rising. I like to be at the office half an hour before everyone arrives. This way I am alone to sort out the day. It is the best moment of the day. Usually, on the stroke of ten, I have a little *casse-croûte,* a piece of sausage and some bread, like the *mâchon* they eat in Lyon. I don't talk about this at home; they think I eat too much! So I eat it at the office with my daughter, Daniele. In many ways I'm still a peasant. After all, when one has lived all one's life among country folk and winegrowers, there are habits that the body gets used to—quite enjoyable habits, too. Now, let me show you the view from the balcony upstairs."

With the mist just starting to clear, we look up at the valley, to the town on the hill. "The rock on which Saint Emilion stands is chalk," Querre says, "but when you grate it, you find it is full of small shells. Descending to the valley and the river bank, the layers of soil change: limestone, rock, and clay give way to small pieces of rock and gravel mixed with sand; then minute pieces of sand; and last, near the river, a fine soil that sticks together like clay. The soil is so fragile, so hollow and soft, that it has been possible to carve from it miles of underground galleries, immense quarries, and even a church.

"This soil has one striking characteristic: it is very permeable. Rainwater runs down the hillside, and the chalk in the soil drinks it in. The mixture of sand and stones is like a sieve through which the water runs without stopping until, deep down, it reaches the water table. The hill is hollow with underground galleries, taking in the water. And every château has drains around its vineyards to evacuate the water. So our vines are assured of dry feet.

"Before spring can arrive," Querre says as we walk through the vineyards, "there is winter. Throughout Bordeaux, while the vines are being tortured by frost, the rows of vines are often channels of dirty water. In the cellar, the rough hands of the winegrower are at the forge working on his plow and repairing equipment. Outside they dig ditches, repair buildings, disinfect and fertilize the soil, replace stakes, and line up new plants."

Querre bends down to touch a vine. "Pruning the vine is how the wine-

Overleaf: top, a map of the vineyard of Château Cheval Blanc with the name of each worker marked on the plot for which he is responsible. Center and bottom, an old vine, pruned and tied.

Mud fills the rows of the vineyard on a rainy day.

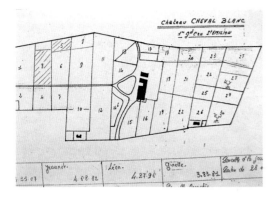

grower decides what his vine will produce for him. As an experienced pruner holds the vine in his fingers, he silently sculpts it in his imagination and prepares the act that will give the plant its 'harmony.' Bending his knees, he will caress the bark, hesitate, and then cut and clear the way for the next buds."

Querre goes through the motions of pruning. "It looks easy," he says, "but it can't be learned from a book. Choosing the branch that will bear the grapes is an art, as is the cutting away of the unwanted branches with the secateurs, or pruning shears. At the same time, the winegrower must leave one small spur on the other side of the vine, so the vine will not die if the branch bearing the grapes should break. The vines must also be cut so as to be at the right height for the mechanical harvester when it drives through the rows in the autumn. The grapes with the most concentration and taste will be those closest to the trunk of the vine.

"I'm a slow pruner," Alain admits. "I'm quickly outdistanced by my workers, whose families have been pruning vines for two or three generations. One can learn how to make wine and everything else, but a winegrower who does not know how to prune is not a winegrower.

"Each vine here should produce about one bottle of wine—one bottle that can be called Saint Emilion. When it produces two bottles, you have wine for the carafe in a bistro.

"We start pruning in December because we have 150,000 vines— smaller vineyards may start in January—and we must be finished by mid-March so as not to hinder the buds of the new harvest."

I ask about the map of the vineyard in Thoilliez' office. Querre describes how each family is allotted a *parcelle,* or plot, of vineyard to work, which carries the worker's name and is passed on, father to son, mother to daughter.

We reach a part of the vineyard where the men have finished the pruning. "And now come the women," says Querre. "They are 'dropping the wood' by releasing the pruned branches still tied to the picket wires. This is one of the rare moments in the life of the winegrower when husband and wife work together. The rest of the year they do not work together or do the same work. The men have always done the pruning, since the secateurs are very tough on the hands.

"The women collect the cut branches, tying them into bundles to be brought back to the château, the cellar, and the homes to burn as wood for cooking steaks on the hearth, or as gifts. Offering a bundle of vine branches, called *sarments,* to a friend is one of those ageless social gestures that costs nothing and creates bonds between people.

"After gathering the cut vines, the women walk the rows of their *parcelle* with a bundle of willow under each arm. Using a strip of willow, they tie each branch that will bear fruit to a wire that runs along the row of vines.

"Willow, growing along every river and stream, is part of our countryside scene. The men go out to gather it, and on rainy days sit around the fire, cutting it for the women amd telling stories."

We reach a part of the vineyard where the vines look younger and where new pickets have recently been planted. "To me, the sound of spring," Querre says, "is the sound of the pickets that hold the vines being driven into the ground: two men pounding each one into the ground, like blacksmiths at an

Burning vine shoots in the vineyard, *above and below.*

Workers cut willows at the riverbank, top.
Bundled willows ready to be used, above.
A woman uses willow strips to tie trimmed
branches to the wires, right.

anvil. Then comes the vibration of the support wire being stretched from one end of the row to the other. In the old days, they used large boulders propped against the pickets to keep the wires taut. A vineyard of pickets aligned perfectly with wires taut as strings on a violin is a splendid sight.

"Our 150,000 vines means 150,000 pickets, and each spring four men walk all day along the rows, testing every picket to determine which ones have to be replaced. In one year, we'll go through the vineyard some sixty times for different work."

Back in Querre's jeep, we drive along a small road, passing the winegrowers' cooperative that makes wines for over seven hundred of the thousand winegrowers of Saint Emilion, and on up to the top of the hill on the outskirts of town. "When the sun is coming up over the vineyards, I like to bring my visitors to this hill. I know this white and chalky road by heart. Thousands of pilgrims passed this way during the Middle Ages. One of the routes across Europe to the Spanish shrine of Santiago de Compostela led through the birthplace of a saint and hermit named Emilion, and so our town began."

As we pass the vineyards of Châteaux Magdelaine and Belair, we see the first colors of spring: splashes of green of the young buds beginning to open. We see a lark high up against the blue sky, and hear his song. "Beneath this road," says Querre, "is the labyrinth of underground quarries and galleries, one on top of the other. At places where two or three galleries have fallen in, the ceilings are fifteen or twenty meters high. When we were young, we would

Setting the pickets, above. Vineyards of pickets perfectly aligned, below.

The pickets stacked in readiness, above,
and set at Château Pétrus, left.

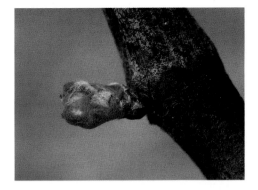  

Above, from left to right, the flowering of the vine. At right, the first days of spring in the vineyard.

proudly explore three or four kilometers of galleries in an afternoon. The vineyard owners do not find the quarries so amusing: from time to time their vineyard collapses into a gallery. Recently, part of the vineyard of Château Belair caved in, leaving a a crater twenty-five metres wide and twenty-five meters deep."

We arrive at Château Ausone where Madame Dubois-Challon, the proprietor of Belair and Ausone, is in her garden. Querre asks her if he may visit the underground cellars. She shows us the way, guided by a shaft of light from the vineyard above coming in through a skylight. The vines' roots from the Ausone vineyards are visible in the cellar's ceiling. They have penetrated the rock on which Saint Emilion is built. "The roots are able to drive through the roof," Querre explains, "because there is a small pocket of acid at each root tip that eats its way through the chalk."

Back on the road, Querre points to the houses in the town below. "While their top floors are no more than two hundred years old, the lower floors are often four or five hundred years old, built with the stone from the quarries under the town. Part of the city of Bordeaux is built of this same stone. Roman urns and jars for collecting grain and wine have been found in some of the cellars under the houses. The Romans cooked rabbit, hare, and goose in their

Saint Emilion, surrounded by a sea of vineyards, opposite. An old stable, above, and vineyard, below, at Château Ausone.

own fat, and then, covering the meat with the fat, preserved it in the jars. We still make our own *confit* of duck, goose, or goose liver in this manner."

We arrive at the square in the lower town. We enter the monolithic church, creaking open its heavy oak doors. "This church was dug out by Franciscan monks over the course of two hundred years between the eighth and tenth centuries," says Querre, his voice echoing in the half-light. "It was not built, but literally dug out of rock by hand, from top to bottom, using the tools of the time. Architects are amazed at the thickness of the walls and the regularity of these arches. The steeple rests on the pillars in the middle, so they must be strong. The church was used, like most churches in the Middle Ages, not only as the House of God but also as a place where distinguished visitors were welcomed and as a town hall.

"Saint Emilion was governed by forty officials, elected under a royal charter awarded them by the King of England in 1199. It was one of the first democracies of Europe. The forty officials, called *Jurats,* are still elected today, but they have lost all political power and the Jurade is now an honorary brotherhood of winemakers.

"The life of our town still centers around this old church—we have weddings and funerals, and once a year we say Mass here. We also hold two wine

A view of Saint Emilion and vineyards from the bell tower, opposite top. Caves outside the town where the saint, Emilion, is said to have lived, opposite bottom. The cloisters of the Cordeliers in Saint Emilion, below.

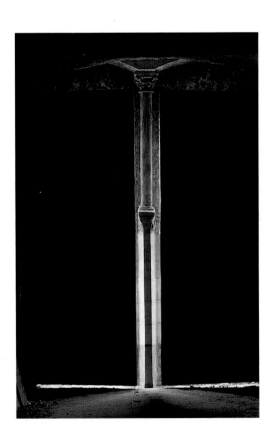

festivals here—the spring and harvest festivals. We have one foot in the past and we try, at least, to have one foot in the future."

Light streams through an opening high up in the wall. "We have no stained glass in the windows, and during the last war many of the stained glass windows from the cathedrals of France, including those of Chartres, were hidden here to protect them from the bombings. Two craftsmen spent the war down here dismantling and cleaning the lead and glass of the windows—an impossible task when the windows are in place. It was a marvelous sight," Querre recalls, "people repairing stained glass windows in a church with no windows."

Outside in the morning sunlight once again, we walk the steep, cobbled streets, passing restaurants, artisan shops, and wine stores (there are over thirty wine stores in the town). We reach the square of the bell tower—which actually sits on top of the monolithic church—and look down on the roofs of Saint Emilion. "Let us go and have a glass of wine," Querre suggests.

We walk to the terrace of the Hôtelerie de Plaisance, recognized as the town's best inn, and sit at a table under a canopy of vines. For this hour of the day, my host orders a bottle of a young red Bordeaux wine, some pâté, and the morning's bread. The wine, slightly chilled, tastes fresh in the mouth.

"Wine is a product of man," Querre muses, holding his glass before him.

Inside the monolithic church, left, and its facade, below.

A resident of Saint Emilion catches up on the news, above. An antique shop in Saint Emilion, right.

"Not so the wild vine. The more the vine climbs, the wilder it is, the prettier it becomes, and the less it produces grapes of quality. The wild vine gives us nothing of interest.

"When spring arrives, the sap rises through the little roots of the vine from deep in the soil. The roots begin to pump the water that climbs up the vine and finally it arrives to reach out through the middle of the leaves, and from there out into the sunshine." Querre's hands describe the vine's journey. "The heart of the earth and the most beautiful object in the sky marry within the vine. And they produce this little flower. Finally come the grapes from which the wine is made, and man is there to assist this birth. And then the wine returns to the darkness of the cellars. Isn't it strange how it all starts in the darkness of the earth and goes from there into the light of the sun for the flower and the fruit? In the cellar's darkness, the wine sleeps. It reflects. It matures. In secret, just as it did when it was in the earth. Now in silence and calmness, it prepares itself. And suddenly, into a bottle—still in the dark. Then, at last . . . " He raises his glass.

"We serve the wine in a glass out in the pure air, smell it, and there it goes, down into man."

Nearby, the bell tower chimes noon. "Time for lunch," announces Querre, leading the way to La Cadene, one of the town's favorite restaurants.

Overleaf: Tending to the young vines, top. A worker at Château Yquem cuts away excess foliage to allow sun to get through, bottom. Tractors descend a vineyard at Château Lafite-Rothschild.

A Saint Emilion rooftop.

"A bistro like this is a place where the locals come to eat, as if they're eating at home." He orders a bottle of Château La Clotte, the bistro's own vineyard. The sun is warm enough for us to sit outside and watch the town go by. "In the countryside we still have our bistros where you eat good family fare: soups, *pots-au-feu, grillades,* sauces, and homemade desserts. Where vegetables are fresh from the kitchen garden, the chicken comes from the courtyard behind the restaurant, and the salad is picked an hour earlier. Usually it is a woman who runs the restaurant and does the cooking, like Marion Chailleau here, and like her mother before her.

"She has made the *confit* herself and is as proud of it as if she were cooking at home. And when she makes a little change in the menu, it's because she suddenly realizes that she has fresh *ciboulette* in her garden. You ask her what she has put in the soup. 'Nothing,' she replies, 'same as always.' 'No, it's better today,' you say. 'Oh, I had a little *ciboulette.'* She does not use it as a shortcut. It is to improve the soup, to profit from the produce in the garden. So many of her admirable recipes are like that.

"And the wine. For you she will bring out from the cellar a bottle that has no label. Perhaps it is from a friend or from her own vineyard. It may turn out to be a fabulous little vintage and she will charge you only sixty francs for it. Or if you compliment her on the wine, she says, 'There, I give it to you.' That's a bistro for you."

Querre orders oysters with little hot sausages, followed by one of Marion's specialities, lamprey *à la bordelaise.* "Marion is the granddaughter of one of the founders of the winemakers' brotherhood, the Jurade of Saint Emilion, which was revived in 1948. When her mother died, there were four thousand people at her funeral. The big church of Saint Emilion could not hold them all. They filled the road from the restaurant all the way to the cemetery near Château Canon, which is two kilometers away. But they had not come just to express their appreciation of her cooking. It was also for the generosity of this woman, for her love of people and her conversation. That was a lady."

At the end of the day, we return to Querre's house on the banks of the river Isle that runs into the Dordogne. After the death of his parents in the 1970s, Querre invited one of his brothers to come and live in the château. Querre's house near the Dordogne has thick stone walls, and the ceiling of the living

Recipe For A Country Pâté

Marion Chailleau

In France people think pâté always has to be foie gras. It's not true! There are terrines that are marvelous and really interesting. But no one talks of them.

Every thirty or fifty kilometers the terrines are made differently. They come from family recipes, so you can go to four homes in Saint Emilion and find four different terrines. We make ours in glass dishes or *verrines,* as we like to take them on picnics. When the mushrooms are out everywhere, I put them to marinate in rum in my refrigerator, and later add them to the terrine, giving it a little taste of truffles. Or I take some noodles and serve them with the mushrooms.

My recipe for the pâté is easy: chop together three equal portions of chicken liver, sausage meat, and unsalted pork fat. Add a drop of cognac, salt and pepper, and finely chopped shallots. Put it all into your terrine, cover, and place in the oven. Cook at a medium heat for about an hour, until the juice rises. Delicious! And after one or two days it is even better!

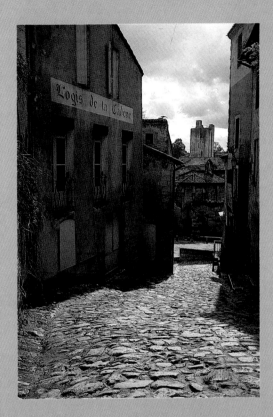

Top, the cooper at the forge. Above, the cellar master cooks a steak over a fire of vine branches. Opposite, Saint Emilion at sunset.

room is made from the frame of the hull of an old ship. One of Querre's passions is collecting antique documents and books on the early sailors—buccaneers and pirates.

This evening he has lit a fire of vine branches in the courtyard, over which he will cook steaks for dinner. Waiting for the embers to glow red, he opens a bottle of young, fresh Muscadet made by a friend, Louis Metaireau, a winemaker in the Loire valley. "There are still people like my cellar master who know how to cook meat—steak cooked over a fire. But if you ask for a steak in many restaurants today, they'll carbonize it. Cooking a piece of meat is a tradition, a culture, the art of a region. It is something rare we must hold on to and not let disappear. Families still know how to do it, but even good restaurants with barbecues have forgotten. If the patron shouts, 'Quickly, quickly,' the meat is taken off the flame even if it's not ready. Or if the patron is not ready to be served, the meat gets cold or turns into charcoal. The patron in a restaurant only wishes to eat well. I'd treat him as if he were someone seated at my table in our house and be confident enough to say, 'Monsieur, it's not ready. Don't you want your meal to be good? Please, wait.' But these restaurateurs allow themselves to be walked over. In a family kitchen, everyone waits. In a restaurant, if you're going to offer a steak like this, you have to be able to insist, 'Please, have another glass of red wine. The steak is coming. It's worth waiting for. And when it comes, you'll be happy.' If you cannot say that, then there's no hope."

A neighbor joins us for a glass of wine. He has brought some shad he caught that morning. "Here in my little village," says Querre, "we live calmly, gently. The neighbors keep an eye on our children and we keep an eye on theirs. They can play in the street and no one will run them over. Everyone is looking; everybody and nobody. They can do what they want, watched over by the eyes of the village. You see how my neighbor here has brought over some fish. If it is not fish, it is flowers, or the first cherries. That is the old way of living. Helping each other was vital in those days. For example, when you killed a pig, there would be too much meat for you to eat alone. You could not conserve it all in salt or turn it into sausages. You had to share it. Today we have freezers and do not have to share. If I share, it is for the pleasure that sharing brings. The sheer pleasure of being together, of meeting and talking together. And when we have our new wine, we share that too, everyone tastes it."

Summer

Under a sultry sky, the vineyard is thirsty and quiet. The quartz in the gravel between the rows shines like diamonds. The leaves tremble in the hot air. The grapes turn imperceptibly from green to blue. The vine is at work.

On days when dark, heavy, yellow-edged clouds threaten hail, the winemaker's heart sinks. A hailstorm could mean mutilated vines, massacred branches, scarred fruit, and even the loss of the entire crop. If disaster strikes, the winemaker will have to dress the wounds—care for, disinfect, and prepare the damaged vines—and not just for this year's harvest, already partially lost. The ravages of hail can imperil next year's harvest as well.

During the first months of summer, the young shoots on the vine are trimmed back to curb excessive growth. The vineyard is sprayed regularly to prevent vine maladies and animal parasites and is given its fourth and last plowing before the harvest to remove summer weeds. The grapes are then left to ripen. It is now a matter of waiting.

While the sun shines, the châteaux wait, too, for visitors. This is the ideal season to follow the wine road through Bordeaux and discover the many faces and façades of the wine country. Because the châteaux are the private homes of the vineyard owners, it is customary to ask the owner for a convenient day and time to visit.

A storm approaches Château Pontet Canet in Pauillac, opposite. Ripe grapes, above.

. . . .

Château Cheval Blanc, along with Château Ausone, is officially classed at the head of Saint Emilion's eleven First Growths. A narrow road separates the gravelly Cheval Blanc vineyard—one-third Merlot, two-thirds Cabernet

The iron gate of Château Soutard, top.
Inside the château, above. The entrance
to Château Berliquet, right. A view of
Château Magdelaine, opposite.

An *aerial view of Château Cheval Blanc in Saint Emilion.*

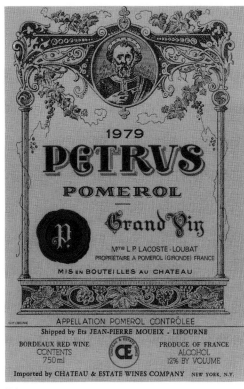

Wine labels from Châteaux Cheval Blanc and Pétrus.

Franc—from the neighboring region of Pomerol. "Geologically speaking," explains Jacques Hébrard, Cheval Blanc's administrator for fifteen years, "Cheval Blanc is more like Pomerol. The commune boundaries were mapped out before the French Revolution, and it was then that it was decided that Saint Emilion should stop at that path for oxen carts.

"The château sells much of its wine to the wine merchants of Bordeaux, who ship it throughout the world. For the top châteaux, about eighty-five percent is exported and fifteen percent is sold in France. With only eighty-six acres of vineyard here, producing in an average year 150,000 bottles, there is never enough to go around the world."

The grapes of Cheval Blanc have what Emile Peynaud, who served as consultant to the château from 1964 to 1979, describes as "an almost explosive ripeness. Their mad speed of ripening makes winemaking extremely difficult. One has only a few days to wait and then, at the right moment, it is quick, quick, quick . . . make the wine. If it rains, the rot comes on fast."

. . . .

Visible from the balcony on Cheval Blanc's cellar roof is Château Pétrus in Pomerol. This small, unprepossessing house, which belonged to the late grande dame Madame Edmonde Loubat, is the home of the most expensive wine in the world today, one of the nine top-ranked wines of Bordeaux. Ninety-five percent of the vineyard is planted with Merlot grapes, some of them survivors of the terrible 1956 frost.

"Pétrus is a small, unique buttonhole of clay—thirty acres lost between the gravelly strips of Saint Emilion and the plateau of Pomerol," according to the château's manager, Christian Moueix, of the firm of Jean-Pierre Moueix, wine merchants and shippers in Libourne. A man of elegance and foresight like his father, Jean-Pierre, he commands an army of vineyard workers. "With an ensemble of sixteen châteaux under our management, we can assemble at Pétrus a considerable number of workers for plowing, spraying, harvesting, or whatever job must be done. Considering the château's small size, this concentration of effort is most advantageous in difficult years. We can harvest before the rains arrive, and we can plow in spring before the big heat. The human factor acts as a supplement to nature.

"The wine of Château Pétrus has a fullness and charm that pleases both initiates and connoisseurs. If one compares Pétrus with Ausone—a wine that I admire greatly, an intellectual wine that demands deeper understanding—one would find that Pétrus is, as my father and I say, *charnel*—fleshy, worldly, full of desires. You don't have to know all about wine to love Pétrus.

"In all my travels," he adds, "I look back and see Saint Emilion with its roots piercing the rock and I see the roots of my family. This was the first land that allowed my family, who came from humble origins in the Correze region of central France, to find its expression. In days of doubt I think about this plateau of rock and chalk that is Saint Emilion, and find my roots, firmly implanted to resist tempests and gales."

. . . .

Château Ausone, on the site where the Roman poet Ausonius is believed to have lived, looks out over a valley in which the remains of a Roman villa were discovered in 1979. The château's underground cellars are hewn out of the rock of Saint Emilion. Its winemaker is the young, bearded, strongly built

Christian Moueix tasting in the cellars of Château Pétrus, above. The entrance to Château Canon, below.

The underground cellars of Château Ausone, opposite. Madame Jean Dubois-Challon, owner of Château Ausone, above.

Pascal Delbeck, who was brought in by the owner, Madame Jean Dubois-Challon, after her husband's death fifteen years ago. "I was twenty-one and had never met Monsieur Dubois-Challon," he recalls. "Listening to Madame speak of her husband, of his personality and tastes, I felt encouraged to make the wine as he would have liked it. My responsibility is to preserve the notion of the soil he loved. I must make more than a wine that pleases me. I must make a wine that pleases the owners."

....

On the other side of the river Dordogne at Libourne and across the Garonne at Bordeaux, over Napoleon's old bridge, the wine road turns right and leads north into the Médoc region. At the village of Margaux, on the right, in the direction of the Gironde estuary, is a narrow road that leads to the avenue of

*Château Margaux, right, and its owners
Laura Mentzelopoulos and her daughter
Corinne, above.*

plane trees that brings one to the entrance of Château Margaux. The château was designed in 1811 by Louis Combes, a pupil of Victor-Louis, architect of Bordeaux's Grand Théâtre. The vineyard's reputation was established a century earlier when the wines it produced became the favorites of England's prime minister, Sir Robert Walpole, and America's ambassador to France, Thomas Jefferson. As long ago as the seventeenth century, its cellar master and winemaker, a Monsieur Berlon, was already making four wines: a *grand vin,* a second wine, a wine for the workers, and a wine for the owner from selected corners of the vineyard.

Like all châteaux, Château Margaux has had its good years and its lean years. In 1977, after a decade of producing less than glorious vintages, the château was purchased by André Mentzelopoulos, owner of the Félix Potin grocery store empire. Monsieur Mentzelopoulos immediately called in Emile Peynaud as his consultant in restoring the château's wines to their former glory. After André Mentzelopoulos's death in 1980, his widow, Laura, and their daughter, Corinne, assumed management of the château. They invested in new equipment and built a long underground barrel cellar beneath the main driveway. (Because Château Margaux is classified as a national monument, no new structures could be built aboveground.) They commissioned a team of restoration experts to supervise the renovation and redecoration of the château's interior. And with Peynaud at their side, they ordered the replanting of much

In Château Margaux's wine cellar, above, and its new underground second-year barrel cellar, left.

of the vineyard. From the new young vines came, for the first time since the days of Monsieur Berlon, second wines, the Pavillon Rouge and Pavillon Blanc.

"At the end of the seventeenth century, the process for making what we call today the *grands vins* was discovered," Peynaud explains. "Until then, wine had been no more than a drink to be consumed within the year it was made. From that time on, in certain châteaux like Margaux, wine could be conserved and even improved on aging. This discovery began here in the Médoc, with the First Growths. They were born First; they did not become First. Their secret lies not just in the quality of the soil aboveground, but also in what lies deep down in the roots that penetrate five to ten meters into the subsoil where they find a balance of minerals and water that will nourish the vine. No one has been able to explain why here and nowhere else we find this remarkable First Growth quality. Or why grapes grown five hundred feet away will produce wines of such different quality."

A *view of Château Margaux, opposite, and the* régisseur's *house, below.*

A *table set for lunch in the dining room of Château Margaux, above, and other scenes of the château.*

CHÂTEAU MARGAUX, 1982

Emile Peynaud

A sublime year, an incredible vintage. If we could order weather, we would order weather like we had that year. From the start of the vine's vegetation, each month, except for August, was warmer and drier than normal. The roots of the vine had to go deep down to find water. Then came the miracle. The first twenty days of September were exceptionally hot for the season — 25° to 30° C (75° to 85° F). The grapes ripened in full sunshine and in great heat. You would have to go back twenty, thirty, or more years to find such favorable weather for ripening grapes. And these grapes, swollen and filled with sugar, gave us, after a difficult period of fermentation, wines of extraordinary ripeness, color, savor, and odor. Wines that we had not seen for a long time. I've been making wines since the 1940s, and in that time I have seen quality of this kind only two or three times. We may have to wait another ten or twenty years to encounter so favorable a situation. It gave us a generous, sumptuous vintage that will certainly mark a whole generation of winemakers, oenologists, and wine lovers too.

The interior of a château in the Médoc.

· · · · · · · · · ·

Château Prieuré-Lichine, also in the Margaux commune, was bought in 1951 by the late Alexis Lichine, an American who was by then already known as a pioneer in introducing Bordeaux wines to the United States. Although he is best remembered for his encyclopedia of wines, his finest book was perhaps his first, *The Wines of France,* written with William Massee, largely at the Prieuré. It includes a beautiful, clear introduction to Bordeaux.

"When Alexis arrived, the château was a wreck and the vineyard rundown," Peynaud recalls. "But he knew precisely what he wanted to do in Bordeaux. He called me in and told me he was going to make the best wine in the Médoc, on a par, in those days, with Lynch-Bages and Calon-Segur. Today his wine is one of the best of the Margaux commune.

"I had high esteem for him," Peynaud continues. "He never pretended to be a technician in wine, but he brought our Bordeaux technology to the Médoc, which, in the 1950s, was in dire need of stimulation. He changed life in the Médoc. An American buying land here raised some eyebrows, but impressed others. I worked for over twenty-five years with him. From time to time we would sit in his kitchen at the château and taste some old bottles with no labels that he had brought up from the depths of his cellar, and we'd try to guess their origin. An excellent taster and an encyclopedia of knowledge himself, he knew the wines of the world."

Lichine became a legend. He was the first in Bordeaux to make his château into a year-round guest house. Of Russian birth and outspoken manner, he was never able to hide his disappointment if a friend visiting the region did not stop first at the Prieuré. "Let me show you around," he would say as if it were his first visit. "You see how we combine the oldest with the most modern equipment in Bordeaux. When I bought the Prieuré, it was a total ruin, producing only about fifteen hundred cases of wine a year Now we produce about ten thousand cases.

"As a shipper and grower, I still taste a hundred to a hundred and fifty different wines in a day," he would say, drawing some wine into glasses from the barrels of the last year's harvest. "The most important quality of this wine is its length on the palate—to be able to taste it for a long, long time. That is what makes the difference between a great and an average wine.

"Inevitably, whenever I think of a château, I think of the man there," Lichine continued. "The man behind the bottle is one of the most important factors in quality wines. Mouton-Rothschild is certainly closely connected with Philippe de Rothschild. There is the Mentzelopoulos family at Château Margaux and Aymar Achille-Fould at Beychevelle; Jean-Eugène Borie at Ducru-Beaucaillou and Henri Martin at Gloria; André Cazes at Lynch-Bages, Lur-Saluces at Yquem, and Moueix at Pétrus. And I suppose my vineyards are associated with me."

· · · · · · · · · ·

Château Prieuré-Lichine.

The wine road beyond Margaux passes through a wild and lonely flatland, past villages with deserted squares, until it reaches the village of Saint Julien. On one side of the road stand Château Beychevelle and Château Ducru-Beaucaillou, fine examples of eighteenth-century architecture, surrounded by gardens, vineyards, and pastures leading down to the Gironde. On the other side are Châteax Gruaud-Larose, Saint-Pierre, Gloria, Talbot, and Langoa-Barton. At the far end of the village, the vineyard of Château Léoville-Las-Cases extends down to a small stream, across which lies the vineyard of Château Latour. Here are two vineyards within feet of each other, divided by a stream, producing two very different wines.

At the end of the seventeenth century, the Ségur family became, through marriage, the owners of Château Latour. In 1963, a descendant, Comte Hubert de Beaumont, sold 75 percent of the family's shares to the Pearson group of London and Harveys of Bristol who brought in Henri Martin, of Château Gloria, and Jean-Paul Gardère, a wine broker in Margaux. "I was responsible for the administration and the vines," Monsieur Martin explains. "Jean-Paul was in charge of the wine and the personnel."

A view of Saint Julien, opposite. Château Saint-Georges, above, and Château Langoa-Barton, left.

An aerial view of Château Latour and the Gironde estuary, right. Château Latour, opposite.

The château required extensive restoration, and Henri Martin had to go to the Crédit Agricole bank in Bordeaux and borrow 1,500,000 francs to finance the necessary work. "We replanted where parts of the vineyard had been allowed to grow bare; we cleaned and relaid the drainage throughout the vineyard; we converted the stable into a garage for tractors, cars, trailers, and a mechanical crane; drivers of oxen became chauffeurs, and we hired a blacksmith, a mason, a painter, and a carpenter. We dug out a cellar for a thousand barrels, changed the presses, and in time for the 1964 vintage, installed twelve stainless steel vats of two hundred hectoliters each that allowed us to control the fermentation by running cold water down the sides of the vats. It was a revolution in cellar equipment.

Henri Martin and Jean-Paul Gardère, top.
Henri Martin, above.

"Six or seven years later, our annual board meeting was held in the cellars of Latour. That evening, while walking back to the château for dinner, the aged Comte Hubert de Beaumont, a direct descendant of Alexandre de Ségur who in the seventeenth century owned Latour, Lafite, and Mouton, took me aside. 'Monsieur Martin, I have just realized that I should have found you years ago.' There were tears in his eyes. 'I will never come back to Latour.'"

Jean-Paul Gardère is proud to have been born in Pauillac. "I have lived all my life in the Médoc and shall never live elsewhere," he says. "I love the vineyards. I love the wine. I love my work. It is my passion. Work is a matter of head or heart, and our profession incites us to be passionate about our work.

"Château Latour is first of all a big family, so I try to preserve that sense of family," he continues. "Each year, the first to taste the new wine—our Forts de Latour made from the young vines—are the personnel of the château on the occasion of Saint Vincent's Day, the last Saturday in January. We celebrate with everyone, the men and women who work with us throughout the year as well as those who have retired. This big family fête starts at noon and goes on until four in the morning. Inviting them to taste the new wine before anyone else is our way of saluting them."

Even though a château can be modernized by bringing machines into the pressing house, vineyards, and offices, it must still be run by someone with a love for the soil. "Our work adds up to a good old peasant reality," says Gardère. "The vine is there to cultivate and the wine is there to make. You hear all the time about 'prestige wines.' They are a myth. It is the *noblesse* of the soil that makes some wines better than others. When God created the soil in the Médoc, and in Burgundy and in Sauternes, He wasn't for one moment thinking about the laws of *appellation d'origine.*"

· · · · · · · · · ·

Back at his own château, Château Gloria in Saint Julien, Henri Martin confides, "At my age I have no secrets. I drink reasonably. I have retired from certain activities, but kept others. And always I have a little more work than I can reasonably do. Also, I travel, because I believe that after you have made your wine and sold it, you should go and hear what people think about it. Just because one year you have sold all your wine does not mean you can sit back until the next harvest.

"Looking back, my 1950 was a particularly delicious wine. The 1970 and 1971 were good too. But the most extraordinary was the 1979. When we were racking it at four months, I had the cellar master draw me some bottles from the vat, something I seldom do. Again at eight months and at one year, we drew off some bottles and drank them. I had never done that before. But this was a wine of such character. My Gloria can be beautiful. An absolute charmer! I have always been in love with her.

"We always need time," Martin continues. "I bought Château Saint-Pierre recently, and we had to start from zero. I could have doubled the production quickly, but I wanted to do it by stages. I will not see the château at its full potential, but my children will."

....

The wine of Château Lafite-Rothschild, a First Growth, was the favorite of both Madame de Pompadour and Madame Du Barry. The château was bought in 1868 by the Rothschild family of Parisian bankers. It lies just beyond the port of Pauillac and over the hill from Château Mouton-Rothschild, owned by another branch of the family. For generations, the two families have been thought of in Bordeaux as rivals. In recent decades, the competition between them was dominated by the Baron Elie at Lafite and by the late Baron Philippe at Mouton. Baron Philippe is best remembered for creating a wine museum in his château and for commissioning bottle labels from such artists as Pablo Picasso, Jean Cocteau, Henry Moore, and Salvador Dali.

In 1980 the forty-year-old Baron Eric de Rothschild replaced his uncle at Lafite. He introduced a fleet of mechanical harvesters, heightened the standards of the already severe selection of grapes at harvest time, and commissioned the architect Ricardo Bofill to design an underground barrel cellar.

Emile Peynaud, who has been a consultant to Lafite since 1975, describes the project: "They opened up a hillside where a vineyard was waiting to be replanted, built the cellar, covered its roof with soil, and then replanted the vineyard! Only Lafite can do such a thing!"

Baron Eric explains the economy of the new cellar design: "Four times a year, when we rack the wine, our two thousand barrels must be moved. Our new circular cellar saves a distance of about fifty meters per barrel, which adds up to some three hundred kilometers a year."

....

A *view of Château Lafite-Rothschild from the vineyards, opposite top. The new circular barrel cellar built under the vineyard at Château Lafite-Rothschild, opposite bottom. Topping the vines at Château Lafite-Rothschild, above.*

Château Haut-Brion, in the Graves commune, is one of the eight First Growths of Bordeaux. The former American ambassador to France, Douglas Dillon, bought the château, in derelict condition, in 1935 and began extensive renovations. His granddaughter Joan, Duchess of Mouchy, continues to watch over the château. In 1983 the family acquired the neighboring Château La Mission-Haut-Brion across the road and installed an impressive high-technology pressing house. The administrator, Jean-Bernard Delmas, produces two of the finest dry white wines in Bordeaux.

Inside A Wine Cellar

Jacques Hébrard

Throughout Bordeaux, we all have the same requirements for our cellars. When visiting the regions, you will see that considerable effort has been made in almost every château to renovate the cellars and bring them up to date. Châteaux differ primarily in what they can afford in modern installations and in the layout of the cellars and buildings.

When the grapes are harvested and brought to the pressing house, they are tipped into the stemmer and, from there, pumped into the vat. Depending on the year, the grapes are left to ferment for ten to fourteen days.

The vats where the grape juice is fermented used to be made of wood. Some of them were as much as a hundred years old. But wood is not eternal. The vats were used only three weeks a year and then for eleven months lay idle and dried out. Before the harvest, they needed to be scraped, disinfected, and soaked in water for the wood to fill out again. And we always had to be sure that the man who cleaned the vats did his work responsibly.

So over the last twenty-five years, we have introduced cement vats, plastic- and enamel-lined vats, and finally, stainless steel vats. During fermentation, stainless steel vats give us the best control over the wine's temperature. They also serve as effective storage tanks for the wine.

At the end of the fermentation in the vat, the juice is drawn off from its skins into another vat or tank, or into barrels. The skins are pressed to give us our press wine.

The evolution of a wine takes place in the vat and in the barrel. In this château, each wine has its new barrel. After eighteen months, the wine is taken from the barrel and bottled. We only use the previous year's barrel if the harvest is small and the oak of the new barrels would be too developed for the new wine. We sell our first-year barrels to châteaux that cannot afford new barrels each year. A barrel that has been used for eighteen months can go on for five or six years before it becomes no more than a container.

To clarify the new wine in the barrel, we use the whites of eggs.
First, the eggs are broken into a bowl and the yolks separated
from the whites. The whites are then whipped up and poured into
the barrel, where they are mixed into the wine. The eggwhites

coagulate and fall slowly to the bottom of the barrel, carrying with them the impurities—sediment called lees. We draw off this sediment by transferring, or racking, the wine from one barrel into another. Three times a year, preferably in winter, we clarify, or fine, the wine. Each time, the barrel is emptied, washed, and rinsed before being refilled with wine. Our one problem each year is what to do with fifteen hundred egg yolks!

The new wine is stored in the first-year cellar, each barrel stoppered with a loose glass bung. After twelve months, the wine is moved to the second-year cellar, where it is stored with the bung in tight and left to mature in the barrel for two years. Then, finally, it will be bottled.

An aerial view of Château Yquem, right, and plowing in its vineyard, below.

"The Graves is one of the oldest wine production regions of Bordeaux," explains Emile Peynaud, who used to look out from his window at the Institute of Oenology in Bordeaux and see Haut-Brion five hundred meters away. "At one time it was far from the center of town. Today Bordeaux is growing so fast that the thirty-five hectares of Haut-Brion are completely surrounded by townhouses. The production is relatively small due to the sandy, stony soil that runs very deep—the vine roots often go down some twenty feet. But the soil is extremely permeable and gets about thirty-seven inches of rain a year. It is excellent soil for vines."

....

In the southernmost part of Bordeaux, beyond the Graves, is the commune of Sauternes, home of the region's finest sweet white wines. Looking out over the valley to the Gironde river stands Château Yquem, owned by Comte Alexandre de Lur-Saluces. The family is devoted to the preservation of the château and its 150-year-old tradition. There was a period when sweet white wines lost their popularity, but this fortress in the Sauternes ignored fashion. Today the taste for sweet wines is returning.

"The first wines I drank were the sweet white wines of Bordeaux," Peynaud reflects. "I was in love with Sauternes in my youth. Later I came to appreciate dry white wines, and much later, the red wines." He describes the wines of Château Yquem as the most extravagant: "the craziest thing possible with wine, perhaps because the châteaux can make the necessary financial investment. The wine is made with grapes left to rot and dry out until there remains only an extract of juice. While other regions produce one bottle from a vine, Yquem produces one glass! Its intensity, complexity, concentration, and richness make it inimitable—that is how its label should read, the only wine that is inimitable. It is the one wine that is more fantastic than the great red wines of Bordeaux. Once, after tasting an Yquem, I told Comte Alexandre, 'You have invented a new sensual pleasure.'"

Château Yquem.

Alain Querre's family has owned Monbousquet, one of Bordeaux's smaller châteaux, for three generations. When he looks to the future, Querre sees taxes and death duties rising higher and higher, and fears that the burden on his children will be great. "No true winegrower wants to sell. There is always someone in the family who will want to follow on."

Most châteaux, he explains, are larger than the family itself needs. "Châteaux were built to receive guests. They are not just there for us to live in by ourselves. In the old days, there were big families of twelve or more, and the châteaux had salons that could seat fifty people for dinner. They were made for entertaining, for sharing the wine, as places for people to become acquainted.

"Many visitors think all château owners are rich and powerful. But there are many like us whose property is small. My grandparents first produced only enough to survive on. They were very proud, for example, when they installed a central heating system, but to make it work, they had to pump water into the attic and burn the old pickets from the vineyard.

"Do you see carpets in these châteaux? In these largely eighteenth-century houses, do you see eighteenth-century furniture? No. Because they have been sold during periods of crisis. Every twenty years, generally, there are periods of absolute misery. That means the furniture has to be sold. Monbousquet's previous owners even sold the carved wood mantels. There is a château fifty miles from here with a chandelier in its ballroom that hangs so low the guests have to dance around it. That chandelier used to be in our château. Later, of course, after business improves, we start over again. New furniture. New carpets. This is life at the châteaux."

....

Among my most memorable experiences in Bordeaux was a luncheon at Château Lafite-Rothschild in the summer of 1977. Peynaud had arranged a tasting of Lafites from 1972 to 1906, and the château had invited three of Bordeaux's leading wine brokers. Lunch was a typical Bordeaux château menu—quiche lorraine, tournedos, pommes dauphines, green beans, cheese, ice cream, and fruit—a perfect background for the three last wines: Château Lafite-Rothschild 1951, 1955, and 1906. They were brought up from Lafite's original bottle cellar, moss-covered and cobwebbed with age. Peynaud reflected on the 1906 Lafite, which he had never tasted before.

"With the 1906, we enter another era of wine, another era of winemakers. Though it has a few what we'd call small technical faults today, it is unmistakably the style of wine of that period. That is what gives the wine its character—a marvelous memory of the *Belle Epoque* of France. I find it absolutely remarkable and even a little moving to taste wines as old and as well con-

Alain Querre of Château Monbousquet, opposite top. Château Lafite-Rothschild, opposite bottom. A staircase at Château Saint-Georges, left.

Châteaux in Entre-Deux-Mers, right, and Pomerol, opposite.

served. They are like women who have aged beautifully—a little *surannée,* a little out of fashion, but still with great class.

"We were privileged to be able to finish the tasting on such a note," he continued. "To taste a good 1955, a good 1961—you can do that with all the Médocs and other great growths. But to taste a 1906, that is truly *la grande classe.* Few great growths can present a wine of this class seventy years later. That is Lafite. People may criticize the classification of the *Grand Crus,* but only the First Growths have the means to produce wines that keep this long. That is what has made their reputation. The wine is perhaps better today than it has ever been. It is there that we touch on the great mystery of wine. Before such wines, we were all a little astonished, a little moved at what this represents."

Peynaud fell silent. There was no more to be said. The wine was having the last word.

Autumn

Preparing for the Harvest

Early on a September morning the winemaker walks through the vineyard. He looks at his grapes, and he looks at the sky. And he says to himself the time has come to begin the harvest.

Throughout the last weeks of summer, everyone at the château has been preparing for this critical month of the year. The century-old oak vats in the pressing house have been hosed down and dried out; the stainless steel vats have been scrubbed as clean as saucepans; the cement vats have been scraped free of their plaques of tartar. The mechanical harvester has been inspected as closely as a plane before flight—taken to pieces, cleaned, and put together again by two trained workers. For if the harvester should break down in the middle of the vineyard, stopping the harvest, it could mean tearing out five or six rows of vines to bring in a crane to haul it out.

In the pressing house, everything from the mechanical stemmers and crushers to the electrical wiring has been checked out by the cellar master, the *maître de chai,* and his men. The vineyard manager, the *maître de culture,* accompanied by the winemaker, has been taking samples of the grapes to measure the acidity level and sugar content. Samples have been sent regularly to the oenologist's lab in town and studied. At the château, the wives and children of everyone at work plan the daily menus, stock the food, and prepare the kitchen.

Traditionally, throughout the region of Bordeaux, the winemakers prefer to begin the harvest on a Monday and to have their harvest festival on the Sunday before. "But that's the calendar of men," says the winemaker. "The calendar of nature is something different. When the grapes are ripe, we must start harvesting." It is up to him alone to decide when the harvest will begin. He must determine which grapes to bring in first: those earliest to ripen, or those

Château Margaux.

Harvesters at work, above and opposite.

on the younger vines? Of the red wine grapes, the Merlots are the earliest to ripen, followed by the Cabernet Francs and Cabernet Sauvignons.

The winemaker must pay special attention to the young vines. No matter how much they are pruned in winter, the grapes always grow tightly squeezed against each other with little air between them. They will be the first to be damaged by rot. The quality of fine wine comes from the concentration in the grape; these young vines will produce three bottles of wine per vine, light wines with little tannin, which are to be drunk young. The older vines produce about one bottle per vine, with more body and more tannin. They are the winemaker's treasure, his *mise de château.* Each bottle will sell for twice as much as the young wine. They are his wines to age. And if there is a risk of rain, he may be obliged to bring in first the grapes from these superb old vines, the most precious part of his harvest.

"Without these, I cannot make my château wine. And that would be—technically, commercially, and financially—a catastrophe," says the winemaker. "In years like '84 and '87, when the weather worked against us, I decided the wine was not of château quality. It was a serious problem, because customers began asking for the '88 when it had just been bottled and was not yet ready for drinking."

In the days before the mechanical harvester, the winemaker would bring in hundred harvesters from England, Scotland, Holland, Belgium, Scandinavia, and the United States—often the same band of workers each year—teachers, medical students, singers, and storytellers. "We corresponded by letter, so we had to determine the harvest date at least three weeks in advance," he explains, "and sometimes we had to keep the hundred harvesters at the château while we waited for good weather—all the time feeding them, housing them . . . paying them. I wonder if sometimes we didn't make our harvesting decisions based on that." Today, with the mechanical harvester, the grape picking can start—and stop—at a moment's notice. If the day is too hot, the vineyards can be harvested at night—by the light of lamps. "I miss that old mix of ages and voices, the time we elected the young Irish girl as queen of the harvest, and as king an eighty-year-old winegrower. Today I have twenty workers in the vineyard and cellars all year round. For the fifteen days of harvest time, we eat at the same table, *en famille,* talking about everything, sharing everything."

THE HARVESTERS' STEW

Henri Martin

This is the recipe for the stew we serve each year to our harvesters. It serves eighty.

The ingredients are:

25 kilos of beef, preferably chuck or bottom round, cut into 2 oz. pieces	celery stalks
	ground cloves
	tomatoes, sliced
25 fine onions	2 fistfuls cooking salt
25 or 30 small pieces of garlic	1 fistful pepper
	mustard
20 peeled cloves	thick bread or
80 carrots	country bread

Lard the beef with the garlic and cloves, and place it in a stewing pot filled with cold water to which the two fistfuls of salt have been added. When water comes to a boil, remove foam with a spoon. While the water is still boiling, add all the vegetables, chopped, and simmer for three to four hours over a medium heat. Add salt and pepper to taste.

Cut thick slices of bread, *gros pain*, and pour the very hot soup over it. Eat with sliced tomatoes or mustard. Serve a young wine from the Médoc.

That evening, with the fate of twenty vats of wine and the livelihoods of twenty families in mind, the winemaker invites his cellar master and vineyard manager to share his decision over a glass of wine at the château.

"I think we must start harvesting," he says to his lieutenants.

"I agree," answers his cellar master, "but it's you who decides."

The winemaker refills the glasses. "Let us go and tell everyone at the château."

The waiting is over.

The harvesters at table.

The Harvest Festival

On the day of the harvest festival, the people of Saint Emilion gather in the church on the hill. Many still remember the harvest sermons of the Abbé Daniel-Michel Bergey, their parish priest for over fifty years. They recall the Sunday he told the story of the wedding at Canaan, at which Jesus changed water into wine: "The wedding guests were all assembled when the mother of Jesus said to Him, 'They have no wine.' Now, if you're from Saint Emilion, you know what that means. For us this water is from the heavens."

Today the new abbé gives his blessing, the choir from the Cathédral Saint-André in Bordeaux bursts into a Gloria by Monteverdi, the church doors are swung open, and the congregation files out into the morning sun. Dressed in their cardinal-red robes and preceded by pipes, trumpets, drums, and heraldic banners of the regions of Bordeaux, the Jurade of Saint Emilion leads the procession of townspeople down the steep, cobbled streets to the monolithic church.

This is one day of the year on which this vast monument hewn out of stone is brought to life. On a torch-lit stage, the Jurade repeats its traditional induction ceremony. The leader of the Jurade asks his assembled Jurats before each new guest, "Are you willing to open the doors of your cellars and your houses to our new candidate?" "We are," they affirm with one voice.

Two hours later, the ceremony completed, the Jurade proceeds with their torches back through the church and its subterranean passages out into sunlight, to climb to the top of the King's Tower, *le Tour du Roi.* There the Procureur, the Jurade's herald, proclaims the new harvest, as did his father before him:

> "The wine bursts from the ground like a flame.
> It is the living force and soul of the earth,
> Bringing life to our bodies, exalting our spirits.
> May its joy overflow and flood the world.
> And fill the hearts of us all . . ."

The trumpets sound. The Jurade cries out "Allelujah!" For the rest of the day, throughout Bordeaux, the châteaux will be filled with good food—and good stories to go with the wine. Tomorrow the harvesters will advance upon the vineyards.

Opposite: *The Jurade of Saint Emilion, top and center, and atop the King's Tower, below. At left, robes of the Jurade hung up during a harvest banquet.*

The First Day of Harvest

A *filled basket, above, and the carriers, right and opposite, who will dump the grapes into tubs at the ends of the rows.*

Across the river in Saint Julien, Henri Martin at Château Gloria is out early the next morning with his harvesters. In his vineyards they still pick the grapes by hand. His vineyard manager assigns each worker a position in the picking formation. Armed with secateurs, they work their way up the rows of vines, cutting the ripe bunches of grapes and dropping them into their baskets. A carrier in each row collects the full baskets, which he will dump into tubs at the top of the row. When full, the tubs will be hauled by a tractor to the pressing house. There, as each load arrives, the cellar master designates its vat, according to the section, or *parcelle,* of vineyard it comes from.

Monsieur Martin acknowledges the apprehensions he has at every harvest, even after over half a century of winemaking. "Last year on the first day of harvesting, I had slept badly and was out here early. I saw things weren't going as they should. I told my wife I wanted to send everyone away. Of course, it would have been ridiculous to try and find new, inexperienced harvesters. I didn't go back in the vineyards that day. But that's the nature of our profession—never a year the same."

At the Château Latour pressing house, Jean-Paul Gardère describes how "the selection of the grapes according to vineyard, soil, and age of the vines is

Overleaf: The hands of the harvester, and emptying grapes at Château Margaux.

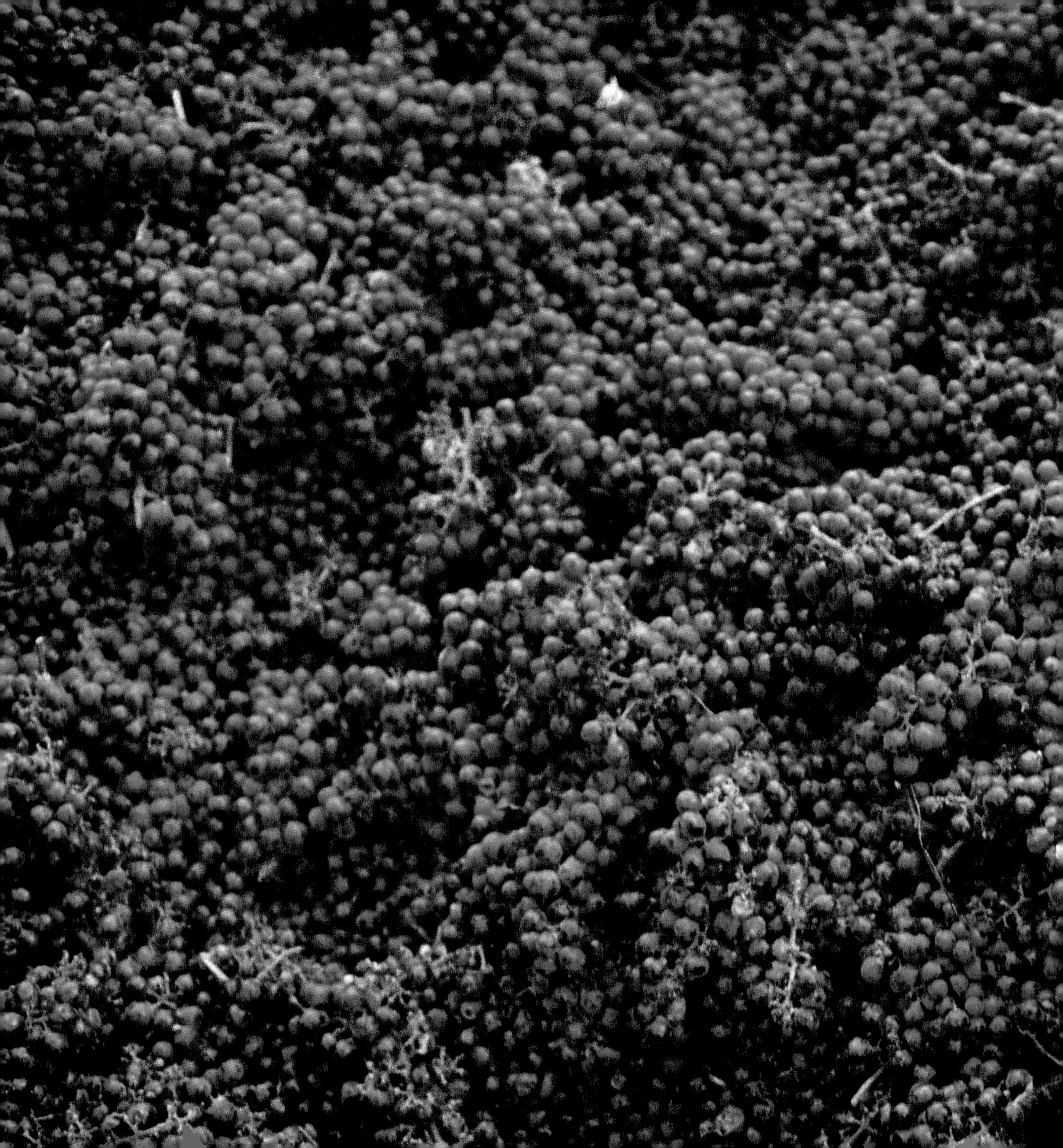

Grapes arrive at the pressing house.

Harvesters on their way to the vineyard.

crucial. An average of about sixty percent of our vineyard's production is bottled as Château Latour and Forts de Latour, our second wine. The remainder is sold as regional Pauillac, or we drink it here as table wine. To make a good wine, you need clean vats and good grapes—it's as simple as that. But to make a *grand vin,* one must also have the *noblesse* of the soil."

So valued were the Latour vineyards that pieces of quartz from its gravel soil were once taken and polished and presented to Louis XIV as buttons for the king's waistcoat. "There's a mystery about the soil that totally escapes human control," Gardère adds. "Just as the neighbors of Château Haut-Brion don't make Haut-Brion, and the neighbors of Pétrus don't make Pétrus, and the neighbors of Yquem don't make Yquem, Latour is something else."

A mile up the road from Latour is Château Ducru-Beaucaillou, which is owned by Henri Martin's friend and neighbor Jean-Eugène Borie. "Fifteen years ago it was the fashion in Bordeaux, when making the dry, fresh white wines, to pick the grapes when they were still a little green and unripe," says Borie. "Now for the last four or five years, it has been the opposite. Myself, I believe in moderation in everything. When the grapes are ripe, there is nothing to gain from tempting the devil. If it is not ripe, one just has to wait. For twenty years, I have relied on Emile Peynaud and his team to advise me."

"Everything changed in 1948 thanks to Emile Peynaud," Alain Querre says. "He explained that we shouldn't try to make Château Latour everywhere. And he defined two methods of making wine: one for very ripe, fragile grapes, difficult to vinify, demanding a long maceration and producing only a small quantity of wine for aging; the other method, for vineyards producing sixty instead of forty hectoliters per hectare of healthy grapes—wines to be drunk young, within three years rather than fifteen. Before that, when we harvested, the baskets of grapes smoked with fungus and mushrooms from the vines . . . they were rotten. We even crushed the grapes in the baskets at the end of the row of vines, using a heavy pestle. How proud we were in front of the girls. But the juice was running out of the baskets, and by the time we reached the pressing house, there was often advanced oxidation in the grapes. And into the vat it all went! Today, with my mechanical harvester, the grapes can be picked and brought to the pressing house within fifteen minutes, and without a blemish on them."

In the pressing house, Querre and his cellar master, Guy Thoilliez, climb up onto one of the vats, lift off the lid, and look down into the fermenting wine. "Wonderful!" Querre exclaims. "When you put your nose above the vat and get that smell of good healthy grapes, you know you're going to have a marvelous wine. If it goes on like this, we'll see a magnificent harvest."

Querre remembers his first harvest alone. "My father had taken my mother on a trip to America on the S.S. *France*. It had been a beautiful harvest and everything was going perfectly. The wine looked so rich and splendid and smelled so good. The vats gave off so wonderful an aroma that you wanted to jump in. And the *vin de presse* came in—all black and brilliant, smelling and tasting even better than our first wine.

"Now, in our château we never put the press wine in with the first wine. Never. But this time, I could not resist. This is something my father would *never* have done. For the next two months, an extraordinary life took place in the vats. Theoretically, the wine should have finished fermenting, but still it continued to sparkle and bubble, and I began to be scared. 'My God, I've spoiled this magnificent harvest!' I thought. But then the fermentation stopped, and the wine turned out better than it would ever have been if I had never blended the two wines together. But I'm not about to do it again."

Grapes for white wine.

· · · · · · · · · ·

On a typical harvest day, Emile Peynaud, as consulting oenologist, has as many as twenty châteaux of the Médoc to visit. "An oenologist who stays in his laboratory, just researching and writing books, is not fulfilling his role. He must get out and make wine. On this visit, I make certain the château is well prepared," he explains. "I check the sugar and acidity in the vats, and if that's fine, then all they have to do is harvest. They send me samples or I collect them myself. It's not easy to do a good analysis of a fermenting vat, so I prefer to collect the first samples myself. After working with many châteaux for ten or even twenty years, they don't need me. I just keep in contact, and if they have any problem, they call me at my office or in the evening at home."

But at one château there has been an accident in one of the vats. The owner's wife comes running from the kitchen, followed by her small children, cats, and hens. "Oh, Monsieur Peynaud," she cries, "we started harvesting and had to

The Starter Vat

Alain Querre

The first morning of harvesting is sometimes a little cold. If the temperature is below 13 or 14 degrees C, the fermentation will not start. Therefore the starter vat, *le pied de cuve,* is prepared four or five days before the harvest begins. A small amount of grapes are fermented to produce a yeast soup, and this collection of yeasts is placed in the bottom of the first vat and the fermentation starts. Though one cannot see them, the yeasts are now everywhere: on the sides of the vats, on the trucks and the handles of the tools, on the hands and clothes of everyone in the pressing house. Temperature control of the wine in the vat will continue to be vital throughout the fermentation. The wine does

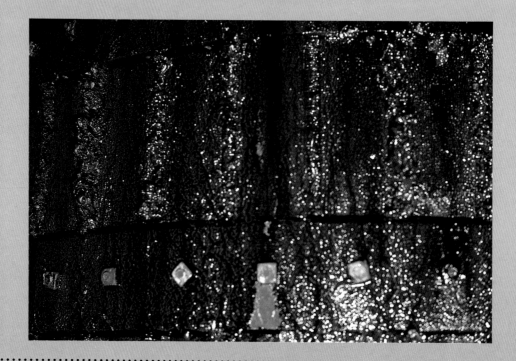

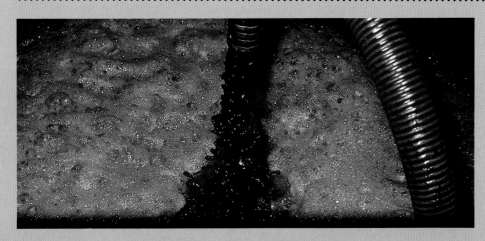

well between 20 and 30 degrees; over 30 degrees it begins to overheat and fermentation will stop.

In 1947, for example, our starter vat wouldn't ferment. My father and I went off around Saint Emilion. At the first door we knocked on, they told us, "Sorry, but our vats aren't ready yet." At the second, they said, "We haven't started harvesting yet, so we don't have what you need." At the third, it was the same tune. By the fourth, we were beginning to give up hope, and our situation was becoming serious. Our vats contained twenty-five barrels of wine each, and if one vat cannot start, it could mean the possible loss of twenty-five barrels of wine. Finally, my father decided to go see Madame Fournier of Château Canon.

He explained to her what had happened, and she said, "No problem, I'll give you four barrels of Château Canon to take to Monbousquet."

"I'm deeply obliged to you," replied my father. "But what can I do you for you?"

"You will bring me four barrels of Monbousquet."

The harvesting and cellar team at Château Margaux.

stop. My husband was away in Switzerland, and when he got back last night, he smelled something terrible in the first vat."

"It's most probably bad yeasts, madame," the oenologist answers.

"I should never have gone to Switzerland," the owner laments as he joins them.

"Yes, one can't be away and also in one's winery," Peynaud agrees as he explains their problem to them. "It wasn't a good idea to put the wine in the vat without a plastic cover over it. Too much air, and the bad yeast produces a smell of nail varnish. Where there's no air, the good yeasts become active and you'll have a perfectly normal fermentation." He gives the couple new directions. Calm is restored.

The next château has newly installed equipment. "The old stemmer collapsed on us with the final load of last year's harvest," the owner explains.

A young assistant cellar master interrupts the conversation. "Monsieur Peynaud, some years when the grapes are ripe, wouldn't it be good to keep the stalks in the vat?"

"I suggest you chew some stalks in your mouth," Peynaud replies, amused.

"It isn't necessary to chew them."

"I assure you it is, because they will produce in your mouth exactly the same effect as after fifteen days in the vat. The stalks have no place in wines of this quality."

Before Peynaud leaves, one of the manager's wives shows him the harvesters' menus for the week.

"Now I can choose which day to come here," he says with a smile.

Peynaud thinks of his visits to Châteaux Léoville-Las-Cases and Ducru-Beaucaillou as courtesy calls. "I never have any worries with them. Monsieur Delon of Las-Cases and Monsieur Borie of Ducru are serious winemakers and we've been working together a very long time. When I began as consultant to Ducru in 1951, I did not have any experience, nor did Jean-Eugène Borie, who had just taken over management of the château from his father. Little by little we both acquired the same experience. Today he does not really need me. We have the same reflexes. And his son has had excellent exposure watching us both at work. His one concern now will be to maintain the same quality of wine."

Grapes waiting to be transported to Château Yquem.

Late Harvesting For Sauternes

Comte Alexandre de Lur-Saluces

The Sauternes region is always the last to harvest. Ideally we need humidity and sunshine; the early morning cloak of autumn mist across the valley alternating with the sun to warm the day and make the mist rise and disappear. We need this combination of conditions until the grapes have shriveled up and reached the desired degree of rot, *pourriture noble* or *botrytis cinerea* that will give the wine its sweetness and high alcohol content.

Since the rot does not attack all the grapes at once, we need harvesters used to working here, who will pick the overripe grapes not bunch by bunch but grape by grape. Some years they may have to pass nine or ten times through the vineyard. The harvest is generally finished by mid-November.

The grapes—Semillon and Sauvignon Blanc—go into the strong crusher, made of hard wood so as to avoid contact with metal, at a pressure of 200 kilos per centimeter. Of the wine from the three pressings, the most difficult pressing and the best is the last pressing, unlike red wines, whose first juice is considered the best. The juice from the day's harvest is pumped straight into new barrels that same evening—usually one barrel a day.

Sauternes is only allowed to make twenty-five hectoliters of wine per hectare—other regions are allowed forty to fifty hectoliters per hectare. If the Sauternes traditions are respected, one has to be even more draconian. At Yquem I have never made more than nine hectos per hectare—one glass per vine. And some years when the weather does not produce the right degree of rot, I decide there will be no Yquem that year.

"Oenology can do nothing for these sweet white wines," Emile Peynaud explains, "if nature and the harvester have not done their work well. All the secret of quality in this wine depends on the degree of noble rot and concentration of the juice; and in the harvester's selection as he cuts the grapes, selecting the best. We are not working here with measurable factors.

"The overripe grapes produce such richness in sugar," Peynaud continues, "that the wine is more like syrup, and some years has a difficult fermentation. Oxidation must be avoided to preserve the fruitiness in the grape. For each of these wines to succeed is truly a small miracle."

At the end of the harvest day, Peynaud visits his last château in the Médoc. The owner greets him with a glass of wine drawn from the vat. "Look at this, Monsieur Peynaud, I've never found it so clear after only twenty-four hours in the vat. What a color!"

"It's always a pleasure to come to your château and work with someone so sympathetic, who works hard and is happy," says Peynaud, tasting the wine.

"That's the Merlot and Malbec. Afterwards, we attack the Cabernet Francs. We have some young vines, too young to have the *appellation* Margaux. You should see them—they're so pretty."

Peynaud's real work with the châteaux will start next month after the harvest, when the secondary fermentation, the malolactic, or *malo,* occurs. Later, in winter, will come the *assemblage,* the selecting of the vats for the wine.

"In the old days," Peynaud explains, "whole vats of wine often spoiled in a bad year. Sometimes the whole year's harvest. It was terrible, but it was accepted in the spirit of the age—fate. Oenology brought a certain security with techniques that were adaptable to both big and small châteaux. Before, it was always the same. The grapes could be very ripe or not, the weather hot or cold, the wine was made the same way. If the wines were rich in tannin, they made hard wines. If the wine lacked color, they didn't vinify as long, and you ended up with thin wines.

"Today, taking into consideration *la matière première*—the grapes themselves—and the character of the vineyard, the winemaker can vary the winemaking. He can make wine he is seeking to make—a well-structured wine, a supple wine, whatever.

"Of course, there are always the detractors. Those who haven't understood. They say that modern oenology makes shorter vinifications, that it makes wines less complete than before. Not true at all. I've made shorter vinifications when it was necessary, so as to make a wine which is less hard—as in 1961. But in general, I conduct fairly long fermentations, as I did in 1975: twenty-one to twenty-four days in the vats. I do that for the *Grands Crus,* like Château Margaux. But in a little *cru bourgeois,* which will be drunk in two or three years, I do a much shorter time in the vats. Oenology has brought a reasoning to winemaking. It is no longer a recipe to apply without thinking. Now you have to be a little intelligent if you want to succeed. I have this phrase in my book on winemaking: 'Only the ignorant make good wine by chance.' To be master of the wine, one has to be master of the vine. Give me good grapes, I will make good wine. You want me to make the best wine in the world? Then give me the best grapes in the world. In a lifetime of winemaking, one never makes the same wine twice."

A *grim day while harvesting at Château Pontet Canet.*

· · · · · · · · · ·

Out in the vineyards, the harvesters are finishing their day. They go home to wash before dinner. The pressing house is silent as the cellar master closes the heavy doors. After dinner and well into the night, the mechanical harvester is laboriously hosed down. Already a mist is falling over the vineyards, and the air is filled with the smell of new wine . . . as if someone had left open all the doors of the pressing houses and all the lids off the vats. It is the big, heady smell of a good year.

Early morning at Château Yquem.

Winter

A snowfall the night before has covered the vineyards of Bordeaux.

"Winter in the vineyard may appear a little sad," says Emile Peynaud, "but the vine, without its leaves, is resting in preparation for the next harvest. Through a microscope one can see the first signs of the buds. Already the quality and quantity of the next harvest is written in the vines."

Peynaud, in the pressing house of Château Margaux, awaits the arrival of the owner, Corinne Mentzelopoulos. "If the vine did not rest in winter, it could not produce that rush of sap in spring," Peynaud continues. "Plant life needs winter. From the heavy winter rains, the soil builds up a reserve of water at about seven meters below the surface to be used by the vine as it grows throughout spring and summer. One cannot make wine in countries that have no winter because the vine will not stop flowering. It produces neither green fruit nor fruit ripe enough to harvest."

Corinne Mentzelopoulos arrives and leads the way to the first-year barrel cellar. A gentle respect has grown up between her and her adviser, whom she often calls *le Professeur.* "Though we may not see anything happening out in the vineyards, what is going on in the vats and in the barrels represents a most important moment in the life of the wine," she says. "You don't see it happening because it's going on in the secrecy of the barrels."

"Some call the *assemblage* the making of the *cuvée,* or vintage, for this is really when we make the wine," Peynaud adds. "Each barrel contains wines from different parts of the vineyard. Like colors on a painter's palette, they will be combined—tasted and classed in order of quality—and then blended to make the best possible wine. In some barrels are wines from younger vines that do not have sufficient quality to create a great wine. They will be used to

Château Margaux and the vineyards under snow, opposite, above, and overleaf.

The cooper who makes the new barrels, above. Each takes about a day. A barrel cellar, right. Barrels filled with wine, opposite.

make the second wine, which at Châteaux Margaux is called Le Pavillon Rouge. It will be a good wine, but of a different type. It won't be made to last as long.

"We put the richest wines, those of the château's best vats, into the *grand vin,* giving us a wine to age twenty or thirty years. The *grand vin* is a careful blending of the first juice that runs out and what is called the press wine, the concentrate made by squeezing the grape skins, which contain the essential aromatic essence, the color, and the tannic flavors. Like spices in cooking, we use the press wine in just the right amount. We make a wine to suit our taste, because a wine that pleases us will please everyone.

"We taste the series of wines, class them by quality, select from them, and, using test tubes, make up a mini-*assemblage,*" Peynaud explains. As if making an *assemblage,* he goes through the motions of pouring and blending. "We try several versions, first with five percent of press wine, then seven or eight or ten percent. We take away one vat, we add another. By tasting, we find exactly the wine we want to make, the one that truly pleases us."

Peynaud goes on to describe how, in the early days in Bordeaux, these calculations were not part of winemaking. Winemakers tried to grow vines that adapted well to the soils, which was a complicated effort, but not at all

Opposite: A glass bung, top left and center and a wooden bung, right. The cellar master takes a sample of wine from the barrel, below. Topping the barrel, left and above.

Eggs for fining the wine, right.
Candling the wine, below.
In a barrel cellar, opposite.

mathematical. Nothing was written down. Finally, they realized it was the blending that brought the best results. "We have known for centuries that one grape variety cannot give a complete wine," he says. "A pure Cabernet Sauvignon wine will lack certain elements of roundness, flesh, and volume that the Merlot can provide. Some regions of France use one grape variety successfully: Burgundy comes from Pinot Noir grapes, Beaujolais from the Gamay. But Bordeaux wines—the great wines of the Médoc and of Saint Emilion—have always been obtained by the judicious blending of grape varieties. Blend a Cabernet with a Merlot and it becomes more complex, and more complex still if one adds Cabernet Franc. The personality of a wine lies in its complexity.

"Château Margaux has one hundred eighty-two acres used for red wines, with seventy-five percent Cabernet Sauvignon, twenty percent Merlot grapes, and the rest a little Petit Verdot. So much for the vineyard's measurements. A grape variety does not give the same production each year, so the wine in the glass may not represent those figures. For us, the growth, the vineyard, dominates the grape variety. Whether it is Cabernet Sauvignon, Merlot, or Petit Verdot is not important; we choose the best. Wine is first of all a château and its vineyard. Then a country. A civilization. An ecology. A society."

In all of Peynaud's written work there is no mention of the word *assemblage*. Nor is it used in Alexis Lichine's *Encyclopedia*. The blending of wines had always been the work of the Bordeaux wine merchants and shippers. Then, in the 1950s, the châteaux, starting with the First Growths, began to make their own assemblages and to bottle their own wines at the châteaux—*mise en bouteille au château*. Peynaud's demonstration on that January morning at Château Margaux was one of the first demonstrations of the *assemblage*. "Until then," he says, "it was like a secret part of winemaking."

The Tasting

"At the professional tasting for the *assemblage*," Peynaud describes, "we class wines that are not yet drinkable and select them for making the final wine. What I should like to explain is how one tastes the finished product, when the wine has been in the bottle for a time and is ready to drink. One might call it the judgment, the verdict. We have been working all this time to finally arrive here.

The assemblage *tasting at Château Margaux, left.*

"When you begin a tasting," Peynaud advises, "fill about a third of the glass with wine. This rule is good also when serving wine at table at home or in a restaurant. Tasting is best done with glasses that are a little closed in at the top. Never use small glasses filled up completely. There must be an empty space above the wine that permits you to smell the wine. For a good tasting we must use all our senses.

"First, look at the glass. When it is not full, we can see the wine's color well by holding it over a white surface, such as a tablecloth. Then, smell the wine: fine wines such as Bordeaux have a very agreeable, often intense smell that is part of the pleasure of tasting. One often can have as much pleasure in smelling as in drinking. Finally, taste. Put the wine in the mouth and keep it there long enough to allow it to express itself.

"Wine is not just for quenching the thirst. It is made for the pleasure of drinking. It is not a food. There is little nutritional value in wine. With a drink to quench the thirst like a soft drink, we do not spend time thinking about it. We drink it. But to find pleasure in drinking wine, we must be receptive. Unfortunately, we do not always have the time. We eat without paying attention, and that is a bad habit.

Emile Peynaud tasting.

"The professional swirls the wine around in the glass with a rapid action so that the volatile elements, which have their own smell, are released and allowed to surge up. You can experience this by first smelling the wine *without* moving the glass, and then *after* swirling the wine. We find the smell of the wine to have increased five or ten times. The longer we smell the wine, the more the smells evolve and are freed in the glass. Smelling the wine again, we notice a most agreeable smell. This wine has bouquet.

"In tasting, we distinguish between aroma and bouquet. The aroma is the smell of the young wine, which we find in the first years. The bouquet is the smell of old wine, a very different one from the smell of a young wine. In aging, the aroma becomes, little by little, the bouquet.

"Taking some wine in our mouth again and keeping it there up to ten or twelve seconds, we can analyze the evolution of the flavor of the wine. The first sensations gradually evolve and diminish in intensity, and other flavors appear—the taste of the tannins. Tannins are the substance in wine with the most taste. At the end of six, eight, ten second, we have a final impression that is *very* different from our first impression. The taster would say that the wine is

Comte Alexandre de Lur-Saluces, owner of Château Yquem, right, tasting with his régisseur, Pierre Meslier, center, and his cellar master, Guy Latrille.

complete, round, and fleshy, with an impression of volume. A wine that fills the mouth. This is an impression we would not have had if we'd put it in our mouth without smelling, if we had swallowed it immediately.

"This exercise gives us what I call the support structure of the wine—its ribs. Additionally, and most important, in the body of the wine will be found the aromatic elements that we call the aromas of the mouth.

"Tasting requires a little analysis. It is more than just saying 'It's good,' or 'It's not good.' To speak about a wine you must analyze it. We can see immediately if a wine has a good balance in the mouth. If that agreeable impression remains a long time, we say that the wine is long; if the agreeable impression disappears quickly, we say that it is short.

"The general impression of what is aromatic in a wine—what remains in the mouth after we swallow—is called the persistence of the wine. We judge a wine by the finish or aftertaste it leaves behind. A wine that leaves a pleasant aftertaste—perfumed, slightly excited by its natural acidity—is a good wine. One that leaves a bitter or too-acid aftertaste is not well balanced. Then there are wines that leave nothing. They may be good wines, but they are not great wines. The aftertaste of a *grand vin* should remain in the mouth for a long time.

A table set at Château Margaux.

"To take away the bitterness found in some wines (which is due to their tannins), taste the wine again and then take a bit of cheese. As you chew the cheese, the mouth will be filled with proteins. Then take some more wine in the mouth, and after a while the wine will appear to have a roundness that is more complete. There is no longer that little astringency from the tannin. Why? Because wines are made to be consumed while eating. The mouth, filled with the proteins of the cheese, has a reaction with the tannin. Instead of the tannin in the wine being fixed on the tongue, it is absorbed by the proteins of the cheese. An agreeable flavor replaces the astringency.

"Tasting is best done when we are hungry. Sometimes even professionals make the mistake of tasting and judging a wine before they have eaten anything. I always say, 'Eat something, taste, and then appreciate the wine.'

Especially with someone new to wine, never serve the wine without first offering them something to eat.

"Like the smell of wine, nothing in nature resembles the extraordinary color of a red wine. It is a fabric of incomparable richness. Though we have not been able to explain its color fully, we know that it is due to substances called anthocyanins, which are found in grapes and other fruit. Flowers, too, are colored by anthocyanins. As wines age, they lose their vivacity little by little, and the red grows slightly browner, with a touch of orange—the color of brick or tile. Then, after some years, the red color is no longer due to the anthocyanins, but to the tannin, which comes largely from the pits and skins. While tannin has no color in the grapes, it does give color to aged wine. A wine with little tannin has little color. Wines of great age—fifty or more years old—lose their tannin and lose their color.

"The purple color in the wine is due to molecules that gain color when they combine. These molecules, which gather one on top of another like a building, are very heavy. They drop down to form the sediment found in old bottles. This formation of sediment is an important process that cannot be avoided. It is a natural phenomenon—and important to explain.

"Sediment is not a fault in wine. It is a sign of authenticity and age. To see sediment in a young wine—three or four years old—means there is a technical error in the wine. But a little sediment in a wine more than ten years old is

Wines to keep.

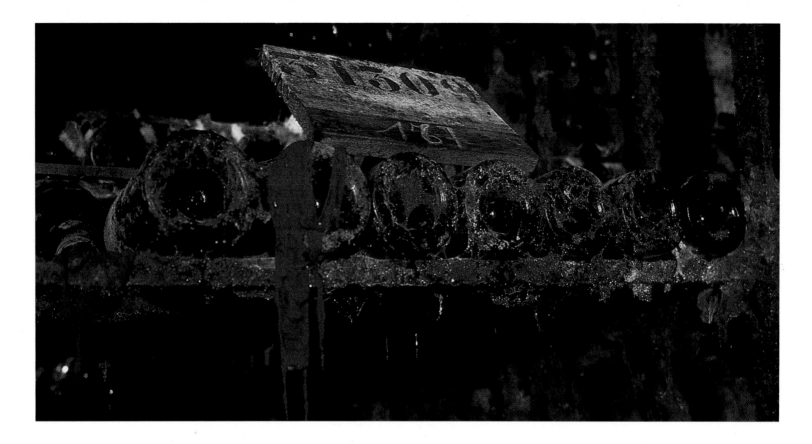

An old bottle cellar.

perfectly normal. In fact, a ten-year-old bottle *without* sediment would be suspect.

"So much about wine remains a mystery—happily, for if we knew everything, it would be very sad. Oenology is still very vague—some things we shall never know. Wines have personalities. And oenology gives general rules, laws, and explanations. But it cannot solve every problem. There are never two wines that resemble each other exactly. But then that is what makes for the charm of the product. What makes it unique."

· · · · · · · · · ·

Alain Querre recalls his first lesson in wine tasting. "As a youngster, I knew very little about wine. My father left me one morning with a man we called Papa Chailleau, the owner of La Cadene, our favorite bistro. Papa Chailleau was a mountain of a man—he must have weighed at least 260 pounds, had big blue eyes, big cheeks, and a big smile. It was nearly time for lunch, and in our house we were never late—when the steak was ready on the grill, you sat down to eat. But Papa Chailleau wanted to taste his wine with my father, who was nowhere in sight.

"'Young man,' said Papa Chailleau, 'since your father is not here, why don't you and I taste the wine together?'

"'Of course, Monsieur Chailleau,' I agreed.

"We went into the dark cellar, where Papa Chailleau filled two glasses with wine from a barrel. He handed one of them to me, and I watched to see what he would do with his glass.

"'Listen, my little one,' he said, 'hold the glass by its stem. Look at the wine. Now smell it.'

"I did as I was told. Being quite nervous, I must confess that I did not smell much.

"'Now taste it,' he instructed.

"I tasted and chewed the wine in my mouth, and swallowed it slowly. I was imitating him like a monkey.

"'So, little one. Do you understand?'

"All I understood was that there was much more to understand."

. . . .

Evening in Saint Emilion.

WINES TO DRINK, WINES TO KEEP

Alain Querre

WE MAKE THREE DIFFERENT WINES HERE AT MONBOUSQUET. WE PRODUCE A LIGHT ROSÉ WINE MADE BY FERMENTING THE GRAPE JUICE ON ITS SKINS FOR TWENTY-FOUR TO THIRTY-SIX HOURS. OUR SECOND WINE IS A LIGHT RED WHICH REMAINS FORTY-EIGHT HOURS ON THE SKINS. AND FINALLY, THE *GRAND VIN*, OUR CHÂTEAU WINE THAT WE FERMENT IN THE VAT, AS ALL GREAT WINES ARE FOR AN AVERAGE OF TEN DAYS. THE ROSÉ AND THE LIGHT RED WINE ARE APPELLATION BORDEAUX WINES. THE *GRAND VIN* IS OUR CHÂTEAU WINE, A *GRAND CRU* OF SAINT EMILION.

THE TWO WINES TO DRINK YOUNG ARE MADE FROM OUR VINEYARD'S YOUNG VINES WHOSE YIELD IS MUCH LARGER THAN VINES OF TEN OR FORTY YEARS' AGE. THE WINES SPEND THE FIRST PART OF THEIR LIVES IN THE VAT. THEIR ALCOHOL DEGREE IS BETWEEN 11 AND 11.5, COMPARED WITH THE *GRAND VIN*, WHICH IS USUALLY 12 DEGREES. WE LEAVE A *GRAND VIN* IN THE BARREL FOR EIGHTEEN MONTHS. OF COURSE THERE ARE EXCEPTIONS—SOMETIMES TWO YEARS IF IT'S A BIG, POWERFUL YEAR. NOT

LONGER, AS THE BARREL NOT ONLY DEVELOPS THE WINE'S PERFUME, BUT being too long in the barrel thins the wine. With the small, young wines, we are looking for fruitiness, so the less barrel, the better they are. The big wines need *bouquet*.

The image of Bordeaux wines abroad, the wines we export, has been one of great wines—"wines to keep," *vins de garde*. But that is not the only image of Bordeaux. There are also little Bordeaux wines—*vins à boire*—wines to drink immediately. My father used to call these "wines for drinking a glass with the postman."

Wines for keeping should leave a long aftertaste in the mouth, remaining a long time on the palate, like the sound of a bell when rung—a long, deep sound going round and round. Wines to taste with the tip of the lips or the tip of the nose. You breathe them in with an immense, very refined pleasure. For the connoisseur, it's the summit, the ecstasy, when one reaches that point with wine.

I am full of respect for the great wines, but there are wines to drink first, before drinking a more noble wine. They prepare the palate. You don't drink the famous, old wines of Bordeaux to quench your thirst. A winegrower also needs a wine to quench his thirst, a wine to drink by the bucket.

Generally when you visit a château, they don't give you this kind of wine to taste, because this is what the winegrower drinks. It hasn't the class of the château wine. What they forget, perhaps, to tell you, is that out of a harvest of, say, 150,000 bottles, only 80,000 or 90,000 are bottled at the château. The rest is used to make the second wine. Generally, visitors never see the second wine because the winegrowers like to keep the image of the château and its *grand vin*.

I am not ashamed to show my small wine. It's better than many other wines you find elsewhere in France. A good bottle, whatever it is, is a wine for everyday. And it helps explain and better understand the *grand vin*.

The second wines can be kept for only two or three years. When older than this they all taste like old leather. Whereas château wines are for keeping ten, fifteen, or sometimes thirty or forty years, depending on the vintage.

I like to drink these young Bordeaux best in summertime, at a relatively fresh temperature, between 8° and 10° C (42° to 50°F) throughout the meal. They go with the pâté, cutting through the fat. They help the digestion more than old wines.

For an everyday wine, you must drink a young wine. And it's worth knowing that all over Bordeaux everyone makes wines like this. It's pleasant, it goes down well and one can drink a lot of it. The price? About a third of the château wine.

The great virtue of an everyday wine is its fruitiness, grapiness—like a good Beaujolais. You might call it a Beaujolais of Saint Emilion. We don't give it a name. We just say, "Please, pass me the pitcher."

"Certain people like to be pedantic, chemistry-inclined about wines," Alexis Lichine once told me. "They stand up and talk about 'My Ph is such and such, my volatile acidity is this and that, my total acidity is . . .' This is *not* what wine is all about! Reducing wine to a chemical formula cannot do it justice. Fine wines have so many complexities. Plus, there is your own mood and the enjoyment that people around you have in drinking a particular wine. This sensitivity is necessary for appreciating great wines. Anyone can build up this ensemble of sensitivities as long as they're exposed to them. Too many people judge everything as black or white. Taste consists of grays—whether it is painting, music, or wine and food.

"People need assurance and confidence in their own tastes. Take away their fears and they realize that ignoring so-called rigid rules is not a breach of etiquette. For instance, if you have a red wine with fish and white wine with, say, meat, that is not a faux pas. It is a matter of common sense that certain wines taste better with certain food. You can have red wine with fish. But with a plain fish and white sauce, a white wine goes better. Not because some rule says so, but because your taste is going to come to that very sensible conclusion.

"First of all, drink the wine, and then, instead of being concerned about avoiding errors, discover the most enjoyable combinations for yourself. Wine's primary purpose is to give enjoyment to the drinker. The average wine drinker is not expected to become an expert. He's not expected to know how to detect the various nuances of wines. Nor is he going to know which wines will turn out to be great wines. He is only supposed to react to the enjoyment he experiences when the cork is drawn from the bottle and from the taste of the wine in the glass."

· · · · · · · · · ·

A *cobbled street, opposite, and evening in Saint Emilion, below.*

Henri Martin.

Henri Martin believes "the dictionary of wine words is not yet complete. There are always people with plenty of imagination who manage to find images we would not think of. When we look at a wine, we see the depth of its robe, its color. Then we take in the bouquet. It is *this* that lets the imagination loose! I know a man in the Bordeaux wine trade who says, 'This wine smells of bananas.' When he says this, he means the wine will last a long time. I, myself, however, have never found a wine smelling of bananas.

"I can always recognize the qualities of one or two of the great châteaux. But when I taste my 1970 in a restaurant in Bordeaux, I never remember what that particular year is like. I'm not so good a taster as that. I don't know what the '67, '70, '71, 72s are. Consequently, I discover.

"The moment I am satisfied, I search no further. Why say 'If I had this or that'? What is essential is to find pleasure in a wine. Later you can seek all the adjectives you like. But first of all, some pleasure. Be happy! It helps you to forget the check when it arrives."

··········

"When tasting," Alain Querre says, "if you are too much a technician, if you look at wine as if you are an expert, or if you study it only technically, you end up deforming the taste. Because one looks immediately for what scientific requirements demand of a good wine. You ask, 'Has it enough glycerine? Has it too much sugar? Has it so much volatile acidity?' And when these have been added up mathematically, you conclude the wine must be good since it agrees with the scientific norms. One tastes like a computer, like an analyzing machine. In this way, a small, ordinary neutral wine with neither vices nor virtues can pass the test, and you will say, 'It's good because it doesn't have any faults.' A good wine sometimes can have faults! Like an artist who can be tough, a wretch, cruel even—yet his work pleases everyone. There are wines which sometimes have faults, faults that make them marvelous!

"Wines are like people—when you meet someone, you shouldn't have prejudices. You should talk. Ask yourself, 'Is the face friendly, sympathetic? Is their conversation agreeable?' Wines are like people! There's an immediate, direct, physical contact that works or doesn't, as with a person. One speaks of falling for someone. This also happens with wine. When you put your nose to the glass, wherever it comes from, you immediately have either a favorable feeling, a sympathetic impression, or a sort of repulsion. First, use your nose. When one finds that sympathy, one knows. It's a matter of 'I like' or 'I don't like.' You don't have to read a book first.

"In general, I think winemakers resemble their wines. Burgundy wine, for example, is produced by the Burgundy winegrower, who is rather large, round, and red-faced. I am drawing a caricature—a tanned man, full of fun, with a cap on his head, and telling big Burgundy jokes. So too are the people who drink Burgundy wine—like the cattle dealer at La Villette meat market in Paris. He has just sold a dozen cattle. He too is big and red. He wolfs down a huge breakfast every morning.

"The form of the glass resembles the shape of the man. It's amusing! In Burgundy, the wineglasses are large and round. In Bordeaux, they are fine and elegant. Here in Saint Emilion, we're halfway between the two. We're a little Burgundian in looks and taste.

"Others are impressionists in matters of wine. They like only the very light, very delicate wines. These are too fading, too old for my taste. I like the *flesh* in wine! Others like wines that jump—the Saint Emilions or Fronsacs, for instance. They don't care a damn if there's no perfume in the wine, so long as it hits them full in the face. There aren't many Fronsacs on the market, but there should be. I'm sure a lot of people in America would love the Fronsacs. It's a wine for Texas—a wine for Texans before they go out galloping off after their cattle!"

·········

Today winemakers travel as missionaries for their wines. Henri Martin, as Grand Maître of the Bordeaux wine council, led the first official delegation across the Atlantic in the 1950s, but not without opposition. "Why would you want to go where they eat like pigs?" many winegrowers scoffed. "But I think of our Alexi," Martin said. "He was like a big ship, sailing the high seas with our wines and our message well before any of us. We and our delegations followed in his wake."

The late Lichine once recounted how he worked not only in and around the big cities, but also in the small towns. "Little by little, I was able to bring wines to the American public," he said. "I held the hand of most of the retailers. The

An old cellar master at Château Yquem, tasting. Overleaf: A view of Bordeaux.

so-called established, well-entrenched wine merchants have built up their businesses today because they paid attention to their wine business. This built up their spirits business too.

"In those days it was all pioneering," Lichine continued. "Only a small minority of the audiences was inspired to become trend-setters in their communities. It was like creating yeast cultures in winemaking, they spread the word in their special way. But somebody had to plant the seed in each locality. People started to learn about wines and how to build their wine cellars.

"By converting the most influential consumers, who told their friends and put pressure on their wholesalers, you could say I was doing it backwards! But when I started there wasn't a bottle of wine to be had in an American liquor store. Perhaps one bottle of Dubonnet (wine to a lot of people) or some Chianti. A wine drinker could travel hundreds of miles around where he lived and not find anyone to supply him. Today, there's a large array of wines in stores and restaurants. In those days, though, the consumer was often more receptive to wine than the trade.

Château Lafite-Rothschild.

"My work was all shoe leather, propeller planes, and rarely sleeping in my own bed. I used to be on the road for six weeks at a time, three or four times a year. And then I'd run back to France and get some more wines. Those pioneering days, when I used up years of my health and energy, were in many ways a nightmare, but in others, a very, very interesting part of my life."

· · · · · · · · · ·

Château Soutard.

One of a Bordeaux winemaker's greatest pleasures while traveling abroad for official tastings and dinners is to be invited to a connoisseur's home and there to discover a wine cellar full of old vintages he could scarcely find at home. Just such a memorable event happened to Emile Peynaud while visiting the United States in 1975. After tasting a dozen vintages of Château Haut-Brion in a host's Fort Worth, Texas, home, he described the last two: "The 1950 is a marvelous, rich, and very vinous wine. You can see how aging improves our wines, how it increases the intensity of the savor. To give a mark to wine such as this would be to devalue it. How can you mark something that is original? All other drinks come from the tap, while this masterpiece is the result of nature and the man who made it. Even the smallest of them is wonderful. I think we must raise the level of the debate a notch higher and no longer talk in terms of marks and points—with this wine we have reached such a level.

"As for the Haut-Brion 1945, we could not finish better. That was the year of the victory, and I wonder if it is not also tonight's champion. Can you imagine something better than this? I am always astonished, when I taste wines of this quality, that one can make them out of grapes. They are so complete, so rich. How do you find words that describe what you feel when you taste a wine like this? I would give it twenty points out of twenty—one point for respect and nineteen for great quality. It has youth, and we all know that aging well is knowing how to keep one's youth as long as possible. So it is with the '45. A historic wine."

Since the 1970s, these travelers from Bordeaux—the wine merchants, shippers, and winemakers—have been joined by the chef-restaurateurs of France, led by Paul Bocuse and the late Jean Troisgros. The cultural roots of France have been planted in foreign soils thanks to these ambassadors of wine and cuisine.

Alain Querre recalls how, as far back as the late 1940s, people were already listening to the great restaurateurs Fernand Point, Lasserre, the *père* Vrinat, and the *père* Bise, "who had discovered our young Bordeaux to be fresh and charming wines for their restaurants. They were unconcerned about vintages as long as the wine tasted good. They tasted wines like they tasted the sauces in their casseroles. Like us, they were men of the soil and of their region. They were looking for wines to make their cuisine shine.

"My father was working at the time with Henri Martin and Emile Peynaud as part of the team laying the foundation of what is today the winegrowers' association, the C.I.V.B., the Conseil Interprofessionnel du Vin de Bordeaux. He invited the great restaurateurs to Saint Emilion. 'Gentlemen,' the great Point said to the winegrowers, 'what you are doing is excellent. You are right to make young wines as well as the old. My friend Daniel Querre is right, we restaurateurs need wines like these young Bordeaux.' And so it was—one helped the other, the restaurateur and the winemaker."

Paul Bocuse roasting chickens on the spit.

The next generation of restaurateurs, Bocuse and the Troisgros brothers, began as apprentices in the kitchen of Fernand Point. After they opened their own restaurants—Bocuse outside Lyon and the Troisgros in nearby Roanne—they would regularly visit the châteaux of Bordeaux to taste and select wines for their restaurants. The great chefs and the winemakers, with so much in common, became visible leaders of taste. And the meeting place was the table. "Many things happen during a meal," says Paul Bocuse. "There is a moment in the composition of the dishes and the composition of the wines that forms a strong link." Bocuse considers a table of wood the most agreeable to eat on and a gathering of six ideal for a meal "because if you cook two roasted chickens, there always remain two quarters of chicken you can serve again." In the wine country, the best place to eat is at the winemaker's table; the best place to eat chez Bocuse or Troisgros is at the chef's table in the kitchen. "On that table I serve a cuisine of the seasons," Bocuse says. "Today dishes are too often unrecognizable because there are no longer bones or other clues as to what the dish is. I see cuisine as something one should be able to recognize. Not an abstract painting."

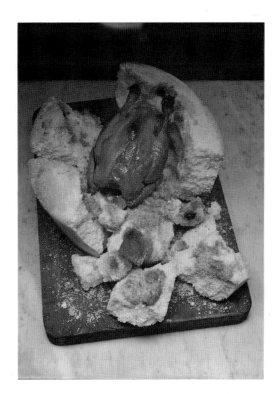

When the winemaker and the chef ask me what I would like to eat, I always find it more exciting to leave the decision to them. One of the great dishes Bocuse likes to propose is a Bresse chicken—an *appellation contrôlée* chicken—raised with the origin laws as for wine, and cooked on the spit over a wood fire. "The cuisine of the spit is my grandmother's cooking," he explains, "the oldest, simplest, most savory of cuisines, retaining all the tastes of the produce." The scene and scents of his kitchen remind me of the cellar master cooking his steak over a fire of vine branches at the back of the cellar, of Peynaud and Lichine tasting old wines in front of a roaring fire in the kitchen at the Prieuré.

"You have to know how to make a fire," Bocuse goes on. "Too many cooks today don't know how to make a fire. It is an art. In modern kitchens, all they have to do is press a button. Whereas when you lay the wood, you have to know how to make the fire. For me, fire is the magic of the cuisine. And the flame. A cook who doesn't see the flame is not in the same profession. There are still some bakers who make their bread with wood fires. It's important that part of our cuisine is still made on the fire. True cuisine is the magic of the fire. Just as

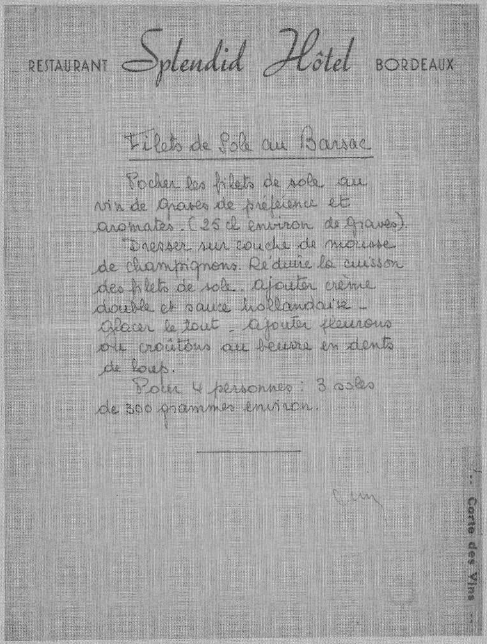

The handwritten card (left):

RESTAURANT *Splendid Hôtel* BORDEAUX

Filets de Sole au Barsac

Pocher les filets de sole au vin de Graves de préférence et aromates. (25 cl environ de Graves).
Dresser sur couche de mousse de champignons. Réduire la cuisson des filets de sole. Ajouter crème double et sauce hollandaise – Glacer le tout. Ajouter fleurons ou croûtons au beurre en dents de loup.
Pour 4 personnes : 3 soles de 300 grammes environ.

Carte des Vins

The menu and wine list of the Hôtel Splendid, Bordeaux, circa 1964.

BORDEAUX ROUGES

Nos		Année	PRIX
50	Bordeaux rouge, carafe 75 cl .... *		250
44	Kressmann Thalrose .... *		600
111	Richemont (Mestrezat-Preller)		300
52	Camponac Monopole .... *		300
79	Graves Lafitte .... *		250
64	Médoc vieux (Dourthe)		250
100	Casque Rouge (Audinet-Buhan) ...... *		300
54	Margaux Sichel		350
55	Tauzia (Calvet) .... *		400
57	Saint-Emilion (Hézard)		400
425	Kressmann (Monopole) .... *		450
468	Cruse (Monopole) .... *		400
60	Lalande Impérial .... *		400
68	Léobourg Ht-Médoc (B. et Guestier).. *		350
80	Ht-Médoc (Schröder-De Constans)		350
70	Pomerol (Hézard)		400
72	Grand Vin Moulis (Dourthe)	1942	400
122	Kirwan .... (Cantenac)	1945	400
127	Cheval Noir (Malher-B.)	1947	450
76	Le Vallon (Hanappier). Ht-Médoc	1943	450
409	Ch. du Pavillon ...... (Fronsac)	1938	450
81	Ch. Rauzé-Sybil .... (1res Côtes)	1934	700
58	Ch. La Garde Martillac	1940	400
65	Ch. La Tour Martillac	1939	600
78	Ch. Malartic La Gravière	1934	900
94	Ch. Virelade .... (Graves)	1936	400
83	Ch. Bouscaut .... (Graves) 1947 *		600
114	Ch. Bouscaut .... (Graves)	1928	900
158	Ch. de Fieuzal ...... (Graves)	1950	500
85	Ch. Pape Clément .... (Graves)	1949	900
88	Ch. Ht-Pomarède ..... (Graves)	1929	1.000
82	Dom. de Chevalier .. (Léognan)	1944	450
56	Ch. La Côte Haut-Brion	1937	900
63	Ch. La Mission Haut-Brion	1945	1.200
442	Ch. La Mission-Haut-Brion	1934	1.200
462	Ch. La Mission-Ht-Brion, magnum	1934	2.400
420	Ch. Haut-Brion	1945	1.800
69	Ch. Haut-Brion	1937	1.600
439	Ch. Haut-Brion	1934	1.600
472	Ch. Haut-Brion .... le magnum	1934	3.200
455	Ch. Haut-Brion	1929	2.500
137	Ch. Haut-Brion .... le magnum	1929	5.000
471	Ch. Haut-Brion .... le magnum	1928	4.500
470	Ch. Haut-Brion .... le magnum	1926	4.500
86	Ch. Verdignan .... Haut-Médoc	1944	400
61	Ch. Giscours .... (Haut-Médoc)	1943	800
179	Ch. Paveil de Luze .... (Médoc)	1947	600
437	Ch. Laujac (Cruse) .... (Médoc)	1933	400
91	Ch. Poujeaux .... (Moulis)	1929	1.500
97	Ch. Cantemerle .... 1950 *		600
101	Ch. Cantemerle ...... le magnum	1950	1.200
479	Ch. Cantemerle	1938	600
160	Ch. Cantemerle	1928	1.000
92	Ch. Montbrun .... (Haut-Médoc) 1947 *		600
416	Ch. Brane-Cantenac	1929	2.500
165	Ch. Palmer .... (Margaux)	1949	800
427	Ch. Rauzan-Ségla ... (Margaux) 1949 *		800
431	Ch. d'Issan .... (Margaux)	1926	900
452	Ch. Rauzan-Gassies .. (Margaux)	1934	950

Nos		Année	PRIX
112	Ch. Malescot-St-Exup. (Margaux) 1948 *		900
183	Ch. Margaux	1940	900
490	Ch. Margaux	1948	900
407	Ch. Margaux .... le magnum	1945	3.600
177	Ch. Margaux	1924	1.800
90	Ch. Margaux	1937	1.800
118	Ch. Margaux	1934	1.800
135	Ch. Margaux	1929	2.500
464	Ch. Margaux .... le magnum	1929	5.000
134	Ch. Montrose ..... (St-Estèphe)	1906	1.600
119	Ch. Montrose ..... (St-Estèphe)	1899	1.800
73	Ch. Calon-Ségur .... le magnum	1945	2.200
95	Ch. Calon-Ségur .. (St-Estèphe)	1950	800
143	Ch. Calon-Ségur .. (St-Estèphe) 1949 *		900
406	Cos d'Estournel .... (St-Estèphe)	1945	1.200
478	Cos d'Estournel .... (St-Estèphe)	1929	2.200
482	Cos d'Estournel .... (St-Estèphe)	1928	2.000
402	Cos d'Estournel .... (St-Estèphe)	1898	2.000
498	Cos d'Estournel .... (St-Estèphe)	1890	2.000
175	Ch. St-Pierre .... (St-Julien)	1939	500
186	Ch. Ducru-Beaucaillou (St-Julien)	1940	700
128	Ch. Ducru-Beaucaillou (St-Julien)	1929	2.000
190	Ch. Léoville-Poyferré . (St-Julien)	1914	950
174	Ch. Léoville-Poyferré . (St-Julien)	1919	950
191	Ch. Léoville-Poyferré . (St-Julien)	1929	2.000
141	Ch. Gruaud-Larose (St-Julien)	1937	1.000
105	Ch. Gruaud-Larose .. (St-Julien)	1934	1.200
130	Ch. Gruaud-Larose .. (St-Julien)	1928	1.800
123	Ch. Gruaud-Larose .. (St-Julien)	1929	2.200
486	Ch. Beychevelle .... (St-Julien)	1945	1.200
171	Ch. Beychevelle .... (St-Julien) 1949 *		900
87	Ch. Beychevelle .... (St-Julien)	1947	1.000
415	Ch. Léoville-Las Cases (St-Julien)	1945	1.200
155	Ch. Léoville-Las Cases (St-Julien)	1937	1.000
159	Ch. Léoville-Las Cases (St-Julien)	1924	1.200
71	Ch. Talbot .... (St-Julien)	1943	1.000
131	Ch. Branaire-Duluc-Ducru	1934	1.000
188	Ch. Branaire-Ducru .. (St-Julien)	1929	2.000
120	Ch. Léoville-Barton .. (St-Julien)	1934	1.200
116	Ch. Léoville-Barton .. (St-Julien)	1929	2.000
136	Ch. Haut-Bages Liberal (Pauillac)	1928	800
156	Ch. Haut-Bages Liberal (Pauillac)	1924	800
53	Ch. Grand-Puy Ducasse (Pauillac)	1941	500
138	Ch. Pontet-Canet .... (Pauillac)	1931	600
103	Ch. Pontet-Canet .... (Pauillac) 1947 *		900
154	Ch. Duhart-Milon .... (Pauillac)	1938	600
438	Ch. Duhart-Milon .... (Pauillac)	1937	800
193	Ch. Clerc-Milon-Mondon	1928	900
435	Ch. Pichon-Longueville (Pauillac)	1945	1.200
129	Ch. Pichon-Longueville (Pauillac)	1928	1.800
77	Ch. Pichon-Longueville (Pauillac)	1929	2.200
491	Mouton-Cadet .... (Pauillac)	1949	600
492	Mouton-Cadet .... (Pauillac)	1948	500
404	Mouton-Cadet .... (Pauillac)	1945	900
185	Ch. Mouton d'Armailhacq	1940	700
429	Ch. Mouton d'Armailhacq	1937	900

(Third column, partially cut off at right edge — numbers visible: 434, 476, 125, 113, 194, 163, 67, 110, 487, 195, 170, 117, 162, 499, 417, 453, 164, 124, 51, 109, 139, 126, 75, 66, 89, 104, 440, 473, 428, 449, 151, 410, 153, 489, 121, 414, 495, 192, 485, 98, 107, 419, 150, 412, 74, 423, 467, 189, 497, 147, 102, 432, 448, 149)

Les vins marqués d'un * existent en demi-bouteilles, majorés de 50 fr. pa[...]

Année	PRIX
auillac) 1942	900
auillac) 1948	1.000
auillac) 1937	1.600
auillac) 1934	1.600
auillac) 1939	900
auillac) 1938	900
auillac) 1931	900
auillac) 1947	1.800
auillac) 1945	1.900
auillac) 1940	900
auillac) 1934	1.600
auillac) 1937	1.600
auillac) 1928	2.000
auillac) 1929	2.500
Émilion) 1947	800
Émilion) 1945	900
Émilion) 1945	700
Émilion) 1949	600
Émilion) 1945	800
Émilion) 1947	700
Émilion) 1945	900
Émilion) 1947	800
Émilion) 1952 *	600
Émilion) 1945	900
Émilion) 1945	900
Émilion) 1950	600
Émilion) 1940	700
Émilion) 1945	1.200
Émilion) 1943	700
(St-E.) 1947 *	900
Émilion) 1950	950
Émilion) 1945 *	1.800
Émilion) 1947	1.700
Émilion) 1948	900
Émilion) 1949	900
Émilion) 1947 *	1.000
Émilion) 1948 *	900
Émilion) 1949	1.600
Émilion) 1947	1.700
Émilion) 1950	700
Émilion) 1949	800
omerol) 1938	600
omerol) 1940	600
omerol) 1945	1.000
omerol) 1950	800
omerol) 1949	1.000
omerol) 1948	900
omerol) 1945	1.600
magnum 1945	3.200
omerol) 1940	700
omerol) 1940	700
omerol) 1947	900
omerol) 1947	900
omerol) 1945	1.400

BORDEAUX BLANCS

Nᵒˢ	Année	PRIX
1 Bordeaux Blanc, carafe 75 cl.	*	250
35 Graves Sec (Lafitte)	*	250
14 Premières Côtes Bordeaux (Lafitte)		250
7 Entre-deux-Mers (sec)		270
3 Olivier Monopole	*	300
25 Graves Dry (Sichel et Cie)		360
2 Le Pavillon (Descas)		360
17 Graves Rosechatel (S. et Schyler)		360
15 Graves Monopole Dry Kressmann	*	450
12 Graves Bouchard Père et Fils		300
526 Graves Schröder et de Constans	*	360
9 Graves (B. et Guestier) Tourny	*	360
23 Monopole (Cruse)	*	360
16 Graves Impérial sec (Lalande)	*	450
8 Rochedor (Mestrezat-Preller)		300
21 Ch. Tourteau-Chollet .. (Graves) 1943		450
535 Le Lilas d'Or sec (Beyerman)	*	400
26 De Luze Monopole		350
45 Graves Dry Sélect (Calvet)	*	400
32 Casque d'Or (Graves sec)	*	350
19 Trois-Couronnes (Schyler) .. (Cérons)		400

Nᵒˢ	Année	PRIX
13 Sauternes (Barton et Guestier)	*	600
538 Pavillon Blanc de Ch. Margaux	*	450
31 Ch. Bouscaut (Cadaujac) 1947		600
36 Dourthe (Barsac) 1947		450
47 Ch. Carbonnieux 1/2 seul. 1940	*	200
4 Ch. de La Brède (Graves) 1947	*	350
517 Ch. Paveil de Luze 1943		400
10 Ch. Olivier (Léognan)	*	400
37 Domaine de Chevalier (1/2 seul.) 1946	*	250
521 Ch. Cantebeau-Couhins sec 1947		400
507 Ch. La Tour Martillac 1947		500
508 Ch. l'Epinay d'Epernon.. (Rions) 1942		400
531 Ch. de Mauves .... (Podensac) 1938		400
537 Ch. Laville-Haut-Brion 1951		450
525 Ch. Laurette (Ste-Croix-du-Mont) 1945		600
6 Ch. Voigny (Preignac) 1938		400
520 Ch. Mayne-Bert .... (Ht-Barsac) 1939		450
515 Ch. Caillou (Ht-Barsac) 1934		700
22 Ch. Climens (Ht-Barsac) 1939		700
509 Ch. Climens (Ht-Barsac) 1947		1.100
504 Ch. Coutet (Barsac) 1939		700
516 Ch. Coutet (Barsac) 1947		900

Nᵒˢ	Année	PRIX
42 Ch. Lafaurie-Peyraguey.. (Saut.) 1939		700
536 Ch. Lafaurie-Peyraguey.. (Saut.) 1948		900
529 Ch. Lafaurie-Peyraguey.. (Saut.) 1924		1.300
500 Ch. Guiraud (Sauternes) 1940		900
34 Ch. Suduiraut (Sauternes) 1928		1.200
501 Ch. d'Arche (Sauternes) 1937		950
505 Ch. La Tour-Blanche (Sauternes) 1938		900
522 Ch. Rayne-Vigneau.. (Sauternes) 1917		950
503 Ch. Rayne-Vigneau.. (Sauternes) 1945		1.200
28 Ch. Rieussec (Sauternes) 1929		1.400
524 Ch. Filhot de Lur-Saluces (Saut.) 1947		1.000
514 Ch. Filhot de Lur-Saluces (Saut.) 1937		1.300
511 Ch. Filhot de Lur-Saluces (Saut.) 1929		1.600
539 Ch. d'Yquem de Lur-Saluces 1933		1.800
39 Ch. d'Yquem de Lur-Saluces 1944		1.800
518 Ch. d'Yquem de Lur-Saluces 1924		2.000
49 Ch. d'Yquem de Lur-Saluces 1937		2.000
540 Ch. d'Yquem de Lur-Saluces 1934		2.000
513 Ch. d'Yquem de Lur-Saluces 1928		2.200
523 Ch. d'Yquem de Lur-Saluces 1945		2.200
534 Ch. d'Yquem de Lur-Saluces 1947		2.200

BOURGOGNES

BLANCS

Nᵒ	Année	PRIX
205 Geisweiler		700
202 Meursault	1949	850
204 Chablis		800
203 Pouilly Fuissé	1950	700

ROUGES

Nᵒ	Année	PRIX
233 Moulin-à-Vent (Réserve)		800
232 Geisweiler		700

ROUGES (suite)

Nᵒ	Année	PRIX
225 Volnay	1949	1.000
240 Pommard	1947	1.000
221 Chassagne Montrachet		1.000
253 Gevrey Chambertin. (St-Jacques)	1929	1.800
241 Vosne Romanée	1945	1.000

Nᵒ	Année	PRIX
223 Latricières Chambertin	1937	1.000
231 Corton	1934	1.000
227 Volnay Hosp. Beaune (Blondeau)	1937	1.200
226 Santenos Hosp. Beaune (Gauvin)	1926	1.200
252 Nuits St-Georges (Ch. Gris)	1937	1.500
242 Chambolle Musigny	1929	1.800
228 Clos de Vougeot	1943	1.400

VINS D'ALSACE

Nᵒ	Année	PRIX
279 Sylvaner (Hugel)		500
273 Riquewihr Grappes d'Alsace		400
278 Kirchberg Willm		500
271 Riesling (Dopff et Irion) *		600
280 Gewurztraminer (Willm)	1947	900
276 Riesling Willm	1947 *	600
274 Gewurztraminer (Heim)	1950	800
272 Traminer (Dopff et Irion) *		700

VINS DIVERS

Nᵒ	Année	PRIX
40 Rosé Sélection Ph. de Rothschild *		800
30 Ch. de Selle, Vin Rosé	1952 *	700
293 Tavel Rosé (de Cubières) (Rhône)	1949	800
288 Cabernet Rosé d'Anjou		600
289 Vouvray sec	1949	500
290 Côteaux de Saumur, Blanc Brezé	1947	600
264 Hermitage Ch. de Thouet (Blanc)	1947	800
281 Léparon, blanc de blanc	1952	400
261 Monbazillac (Réserve)	1949	950

Nᵒ	Année	PRIX
262 Côtes de Provence, blanc de blanc	1952	800
292 Ch. de Panisseau, blanc de blanc, sec *		350
267 Châteauneuf du Pape	1945	900
268 Châteauneuf du Pape	1947 *	800
291 Côte Rôtie (Rhône)	1943	700
263 Liebfraumilch (Rhin)	1948	900
300 Beyerman Extra-Dry		600
350 Ackerman Brut	1948	800

CHAMPAGNES

Nᵒ	Année	PRIX
319 Delbeck (Brut)	1947 *	1.900
328 Ruinart (Brut)	1945	1.900
315 Ruinart, rés. de Rothschild (Brut)	1943	2.200
338 Taittinger (Blanc de blanc, Brut)	1949	2.000
321 Deutz (Brut)	1945	1.900
308 G. Goulet (Brut)	1947 *	1.900
306 Ayala (Brut)	1947	1.900
324 Pommery Drapeau (Sec) *		1.800

Nᵒ	Année	PRIX
325 Pommery (Brut)	1947	2.000
304 Castellane (Brut)	1947	1.900
310 Rœderer (Brut)	1947	2.000
309 Lanson (Brut)	1949 *	2.000
336 Perrier-Jouët (Brut)	1947	2.000
317 Mumm Cordon Rouge .... (Brut)	1949	2.000
341 Moët et Chandon (Brut)	1949	2.000
323 Moët et Chandon Dom Pérignon	1943	3.000

Nᵒ	Année	PRIX
301 Charles Heidsieck (Brut)	1947	2.000
322 Irroy (Brut)	1947	2.000
312 Veuve Clicquot (Brut)	1949	2.000
318 Veuve Clicquot, magnum (Brut)	1947	4.000
337 Veuve Clicquot rosé .... (Brut)	1943	2.500
316 Pol Roger (Brut)	1942	2.000
342 Krug (Brut)		2.000
333 Bollinger (Brut)	1945	2.200

Tous les vins de châteaux sont mis en bouteille à la propriété

the true winegrower has to know the art of pruning the vine, the chef has to know how to make a fire.

"Before the roast chicken," he suggests, "a good soup is truly fantastic. I adore soups, but they have become forgotten these days. For a good cuisine, you need good produce—good vegetables. On the hillside behind the restaurant, we cultivate our own vegetables. This morning, before the sun had risen, my gardeners gathered the vegetables, with all the freshness of the night still on them. People today want everything and want it all year round. We tend to forget the seasons, and that is regrettable."

....

At times when I reflect on my conversations with winemakers over the years, often at dinnertime in their homes, I find myself imagining an evening with all of us gathered around a large table, a table of friends. As always, *they* have brought the wines. And I have brought two of my longtime friends to join us: Robert Mondavi, the winemaker from the Napa Valley, and the incomparable food writer M.F.K. Fisher, who, like me, went to France and stayed and stayed.

Paul Bocuse welcomes everyone, describing the roast chicken he is going to prepare, "a simple dish that can also be a *grand plat,* so we can decide which wines we'd like, depending on the quality of the chicken and the quality of the cooking. After all, we are here in Bordeaux, a country of vineyards. I would love to start with an Yquem served chilled as an aperitif with *foie gras.*"

"You can see why, when dining at one of the great French chefs, I have quivers of excitement," says Alexis Lichine. "There is a such a sense of anticipation, of great expectations. Sometimes I build a dinner around the wine I feel most like having. If I'm tired, I may not feel up to the appreciation, concentration, and complexities of the finer wines with their fantastic array of tastes, like a peacock's tail. To fathom out all these complexities of taste, you need to feel fresh. So perhaps that evening you serve a red Bordeaux that is young and good company."

"If you had to introduce an alien, a complete stranger to the earth, to wine, where would you start?" one of us asks Emile Peynaud.

"Easy," he replies. "I would simply give him a glass of wine to taste, and with that he would become a human being!"

*Château
Lafite-Rothschild.*

"With amusing conversation, when everything is going well," M.F.K. Fisher says with a smile, "it's fun just to put your elbows on the table and go on talking instead of breaking, moving over to the fireplace or to another room. I like to sit at the table."

The smells from Bocuse's fire add to the guests' pleasure. "Cabernet Sauvignon vines make the best fire," declares Henri Martin.

"They make better embers for cooking steaks," adds Jean-Paul Gardère.

"You both sound so authoritative," says a smiling Jean-Pierre Moueix. "Now I understand why we in Saint Emilion hear so much talk about the *grillades,* the steaks cooked on the grill in the Médoc. It is because of your Cabernet Sauvignon."

"Try it, Monsieur Moueix," recommends Henri Martin. "Burn three different vines and see the difference in the heat, the embers, and the size of the fire after using Cabernet Sauvignon vines."

The last wine of the evening, an older vintage of Yquem, is served. "This Yquem is so sensual it is like the extract of an ideal wine," comments Peynaud.

"A wine to drink with a beautiful woman," says Gardère.

"Yes," says Peynaud, "Yquem was invented for evenings together like this one."

"And with it," M.F.K. Fisher suggests, "I see ripe peaches and some wonderfully ripe muscat grapes."

Moments of the evening's delicious conversation float up from the table and hang in the air, like the aftertaste, the finish of a wine.

"Our wines have a common language and are enjoyed the world over," Bob Mondavi adds. "I have learned a tremendous amount from Monsieur Peynaud. He has set the pace for winemaking not only in France, but throughout the world. I want to thank you, Emile, for all you have done to make stars of us winemakers. Thank you very much."

Candles, brought to the table to replace the electric light, remind Jean-Eugène Borie of the days of his grandfather. "We were all very economical, and if we didn't need lights, we were happy just resting by the light of the logs burning in the fireplace. Our children were four or five then, but they still remember well these evenings. We relaxed. It was called the *veillée,* meaning the evening watch. The time when country folk rested together around the fireplace. With no newspapers, radio, or television, they told stories about

Lunch set for two in the library at Château Margaux, opposite. The dining room at Château Saint-Pierre, above.

Château Lafite-Rothschild.

what had happened that day. Amusing, well-told stories, which they improved and added to as they told them."

"Jean-Eugène is like our friend Mr. Mondavi," says Henri Martin, rising to propose the evening's toast. "He likes what he does and he does it with a lot of love. It is a very difficult profession, with risks like frosts and hail, or rain at harvest time. If one doesn't love this profession, it's better not to be in it.

"Jean-Eugène's family has been attached to the soil for a long time. He has the good fortune of still having his wonderful wife and their children near him. With that you can build something solid. When you taste the '64 Ducru-Beaucaillou, you are in contact with a beautiful family and a fine, full, deep-colored wine. A wine given time. Recently," Martin recounts, "Jean-Eugène and I were traveling in the Far East and were wonderfully surprised, when at the same dinner in Hong Kong we were served both my 1966 Gloria and his extraordinary '64 Ducru. When you are a long, long way from home like that, your own bottle, your own label is like a small flag that recalls your country. It makes your heart feel warm. This Ducru is a wine in which you can have confidence in the future. It is relatively young. And if you have a rendezvous with it in twenty years, it will still be there. And I hope that we are too."

....

"My house is a sacred place," Alain Querre once said to me. "For me to share my food is, forgive the expression, a little like sharing a bed. We are tasting voluptuous things, talking as we eat, talking of anything we wish. This is a true table of friends, for I believe the best seasoning for a dish is friendship."

As we strolled across the lawn of his château that evening, we could hear the sound of the water along the water's edge. "I like this perfect calm, listening to the insects in the air, the crickets and the frogs, even the sound of the train in the distance. Then, perfect silence.

"I remember an evening when I was eighteen years old," Querre said. "My father and I set off on a walk through the medieval town of Saint Emilion, talking in the moonlight. He told me stories of his youth. I told him of mine. We spoke of many things — until three in the morning. I will always remember the light of the moon on the roofs of those medieval buildings. The next day we stood in the bright daylight in front our eighteenth-century château, its façade so severe, so rigorous, so very rational. At that moment I first understood that life is not just dreaming. It is also reasoning. My father said nothing at all. He simply showed me the Gothic in the moonlight and the château in full sunlight. The whole story lies there."

Bespaloff, Alexis. *New Signet Book of Wine.* New York: Simon & Schuster, 1986.

Bespaloff, Alexis. *Schoonmaker Encyclopedia of Wines.* New York: William Morrow, 1988.

Bocuse, Paul. *La Cuisine du Marché.* Paris: Flammarion et Cie, 1976.

Bocuse, Paul. *Paul Bocuse's French Cooking.* New York: Pantheon Books, 1977.

Faith, Nicholas. *Châteaux Margaux.* Paris: Flammarion et Cie, 1988.

Fisher, M.F.K. *The Art of Eating.* New York: Alfred A. Knopf, 1954.

Fisher, M.F.K. *As They Were.* New York: Alfred A. Knopf, 1955.

Guillard, Michel and Jean Lacouture. *Le Pieton de Bordeaux.* Bordeaux: ACE, 1981.

Guillard, Michel. *Châteaux Bordeaux.* Catalogue of Châteaux of Bordeaux Exhibition at Centre Pompidou. Paris, 1988.

Guillard, Michel. *Couleur France.* Paris: Editions du Chine, 1988.

Guillard, Michel. *Médoc, presqu'ile du vin.* Texts by Emile Peynaud, Jean Lacouture, P. Veilletet. Paris: ACE, 1982.

Johnson, Hugh. *Modern Encyclopedia of Wine.* New York: Simon & Schuster, 1983.

Johnson, Hugh. *Vintage.* New York: Simon & Schuster, 1989.

Johnson, Hugh. *World Atlas of Wine.* New York: Simon & Schuster, 1987.

Lichine, Alexis. *Encyclopedia of Wines & Spirits.* New York: Alfred A. Knopf, 1989.

Lichine, Alexis. *Guide to the Wines & Vineyards of France.* New York: Alfred A. Knopf, 1989.

Lichine, Alexis, with William E. Massee. *The Wines of France.* New York: Alfred A. Knopf, 1951.

Olney, Richard, with Michel Guillard. *Yquem.* Boston: David R. Godine, 1985.

Peynaud, Emile. *Knowing & Making Wine.* New York: John Wiley & Sons, 1984.

Peynaud, Emile. *Les Vins et Ses Jours.* Paris: Bordas, 1989.

Peynaud, Emile. *The Taste of Wine.* London: Macdonald & Co., 1987.

Sichel, Peter M.F. *Which Wine?* New York: Harper & Row, 1975.

Troisgros, Jean and Pierre. *The Chefs of Roanne.* New York: William Morrow, 1980.

To my friends, the chefs and restaurateurs: Paul Bocuse, Jean and Pierre Troisgros, Roger Verge, Jean-Pierre and Paul Haeberlin, André Soltner, Jean-Louis Palladin, and the many others who have played a role or been behind the scenes, my sincere appreciation and love:

Michel and Catherine Guillard and the team at Scope and *l'Amateur de Bordeaux.* Monica and Ronald Searle; Valerios Caloutsis; Jean Vilar, Maria Casares, Gerard Philipe, Micheline Rozan, Maurice Jarre, Théâtre National Populaire; Jacques Esterel; Jacques Canetti; Catherine Rouvel; Dan Sturge-Moore, Radio-Diffusion-Télèvision-Française. Douglas Fairbanks, Jr.; H. Sichel & Sons; Restaurant Lutece; Milton Goldman, ICM; Sam and Michael Aaron, Sherry-Lehmann; Abdallah H. Simon, Château & Estate Wines; Charles Mueller and Gerard Yvernault, Kobrand, Inc.; Edward Stanton; Julius Wile; Warren B. Strauss; Paul Kovi and Tom Margittai, Four Seasons Restaurant; Kevin Zraly, Windows on the World Restaurant; Frank Prial; Edwin Newman; Sidney Offit; Jean Rowan; George Troisgros; Liv Ullmann; Doris Tobias;

Eunice Fried; Harriet and Bill Lembeck; Alexis Bespaloff; Barbara Ensrud; Mary Mulligan; Marvin Shanken, The Wine Spectator; Dorothy Cann, French Culinary Institute; Jules Epstein; Robert Misch; Frank and Maurice Feinberg; John Rapp; Tony Aviles; Philip Seldon, *Vintage* Magazine; Ron Fonte, Les Amis du Vin; John Digby; Peter Sheahan; Pan American World Airways; David Rosengarten and Josh Wesson, The Wine & Food Companion; Victor Wdowiak and Sidney Sigel; Ron Monessin and Jean Laffont, Restaurant Oz; Larry and Marcia Herndon; Don Saffran. Richard Trabulsi Sr. & Jr. and Henry Kucharzik, Richards; Robert Sakowitz; André Crispin. Dr. Marvin Overton. Gregory Thomas, Grand Maître, Commanderie de Bordeaux; Dr. Louis Skinner. Howard Nason. Sidney and Eileen Walkenstein, Russell Baum; Sheldon Margolis; Andy Fruzzetti; Carolyn Johnson. M.F.K. Fisher; Robert and Michael Mondavi. Hugh Johnson; Frank Dunlop; Marius Goring; Jean Marsh; Peter Shamash; Harry Waugh; General Sir William Platt; Winifred Buller.